BEYOND THE BASICS

樂 在 溝 通

Communicative Chinese
for Intermediate/Advanced Learners

Authors: Jianhua Bai, Ruyu Sung, Janet Zhiqun Xing

作者：白建華、宋如瑜、邢志羣

Editor: Janet Zhiqun Xing

編輯：邢志羣

Cheng & Tsui Company

First edition

Cheng & Tsui Company
25 West Street
Boston, MA 02111-1268 USA
e-mail: ct@world.std.com
WWW: http://hoshi.cic.sfu.ca/cheng-tsui

Library of Congress Catalog Card Number: 96-84640

ISBN: 0-88727-226-6

Printed in the United States of America

PUBLISHER'S NOTE

The Cheng & Tsui Company is pleased to announce the most recent volume of its Asian Language Series, *Beyond the Basics: Communicative Chinese for Intermediate/Advanced Learners*. Designed for intermediate to advanced level students of Mandarin Chinese, this textbook emphasizes spoken competence through thought-provoking conversational topics that encourage serious dialogue among students.

The *C&T Asian Language Series* is designed to publish and widely distribute quality language texts as they are completed by such leading institutions as the Beijing Language Institute, as well as other significant works in the field of Asian languages developed in the United States and elsewhere.

We welcome readers' comments and suggestions concerning the publications in this series. Please contact the following members of the Editorial Board:

Professor Shou-hsin Teng, Chief Editor
Dept. of Asian Languages and Literature
University of Massachusetts, Amherst, MA 01003

Professor Samuel Cheung
Dept. of East Asian Languages
University of California
Berkeley, CA 94720

Professor Ying-che Li
Dept. of East Asian Languages
University of Hawaii
Honolulu, HI 96822

Professor Timothy Light
Dept. of Religion
Western Michigan University
Kalamazoo, MI 49008

Professor Ronald Walton
Dept. of Hebrew and East Asian Languages and Literature
University of Maryland, College Park, MD 20742

ABOUT THE AUTHORS

Janet Zhiqun Xing is Assistant Professor in the Program of Asian Studies, University of Vermont.

Juanhua Bai is Assistant Professor in the Department of Modern Languages and Literature, Kenyon College.

Juyu Sung is with the Inter-University Program for Chinese Language Studies in Taipei administered by Stanford University.

ACKNOWLEDGMENTS

With the publication of this book, we wish to express our special thanks to Professor Scott McGinnis and Professor Ronald Walton at The University of Maryland for their valuable comments on the earlier manuscript, to Professor Richard Chi and the students (1994-1995) of the Chinese Summer School at Middlebury College who used this book and gave us tremendous encouragement to publish it. Our thanks also go to Professor Hesheng Zhang at Beijing Normal University for his comments on part of the manuscript, to Xia Liang, Fang Liu, and Hesheng Zhang for recording the lessons, and to Professor James Dew for sorting the vocabulary index. We are very grateful to Ms. Lori D. Ainbinder at Cheng & Tsui Company for editing the English and for giving us many constructive suggestions about the format of the text and to Dr. Peter Leimbigler at Asian Communications Québec Inc. for helping us with the technical problems related to the Chinese software used for this project. Last, but not least, we want to thank the University of Vermont and Kenyon College for funding part of our research.

Janet Zhiqun Xing

邢 志 群

University of Vermont
February, 1996

ABBREVIATIONS AND SYMBOLS

ADJ.	adjective; stative verb*
ADJ.P.	adjective phrase
ADV.	adverb
ADV.P.	adverbial phrase
ASP.	aspect marker
AUX.	auxiliary
CAUS.	causative marker
CL.	measure word or classifier
COLLOQ.	colloquialism
LIT.	literal translation
N.	(proper) noun
NP	noun phrase
P.	phrase/preposition
P.P.	prepositional phrase
S.	sentence
V.	verb
V.P.	verb phrase
CONJ.	conjunction
(X)	X is optional or X is further explanation
X/Y	either X or Y

*Some Chinese adjectives can also be used as stative verbs. In this case, they are glossed as "(to be) adj."

Note:

1. Every new character in this book is given with its original tone. Tone changes (for instance: a third-third tone phrase should be changed to a second-third tone) are not marked for the new characters, because students are easily confused as to whether the given tone is the character's original tone or changed one.

2. The part of speech is given for all of the new words in each chapter. If a word can be used, for instance, as both a noun and a verb, both functions are given regardless of whether they both occur in the text. And the function that used in the text always precedes the one that is not used in the text.

INTRODUCTION

This book aims to develop competence in advanced Chinese with an emphasis on the improvement of spoken language skills. It is designed for students who have studied for two years in a regular college program.

The book reflects our belief that foreign language teachers should not blindly follow any particular approach or method. We need to be aware of the advantages and disadvantages of the various methods employed by all the contributing disciplines, and we should also consider the characteristics of the learner, the learning task, and the whole situation in which learning occurs. We have incorporated research from different disciplines into the design and development of this book.

The foreign language profession has been influenced by many disciplines, such as linguistics, psychology, sociology, computer science etc. As new theories emerge in these disciplines we find one method succeeding another in popularity in foreign language publications: Grammar-translation Method, Direct Method, Audiolingual Approach, the Silent Way, the Communicative Teaching Method, Suggestopedia, the Natural Approach, the Proficiency Movement, and Computer-Assisted Language Learning. Unfortunately, foreign language teaching is often a child of fashion following these other disciplines. What is needed is for scholars in the foreign language teaching profession to create their own autonomous discipline which uses related sciences instead of being used by them. In the next section we will discuss some of the principles that guide our writing of this book.

Encourage Constant Meaningful Communication

The materials and activities in this book are designed to help students actively engage in constant meaningful communication within various contexts.

We believe that the classroom should be an efficient place to facilitate language learning, and the teacher should provide optimal input, which should be comprehensible, interesting, and relevant, as well as of sufficient quantity. But exposure to this input alone is insufficient – it is essential to provide opportunities for students to become actively involved; however, frequent repetition of the same activity is often difficult for adult foreign language learners, because overlearning through repetitious activities often causes distaste on the part of the learner. Consequently, it is important for teachers to design various learning activities which encourage active, meaningful communication instead of teaching about the discrete skills of the language.

Meet Individual Characteristics and Needs

Students come from different backgrounds, differ in cognitive styles, and have different needs. In this book, we try to meet individual needs by providing a large pool of supplementary vocabulary. We do not expect every student to remember all the words we provide. The reason we provide so many words for each chapter is to meet students' needs in terms of content areas. We also provide a variety of communicative activities and suggest teaching procedures in accordance with our students' learning styles.

Contextualize Linguistic Patterns

In this book, linguistic patterns are contextualized and explained in terms of function as well as structure. New patterns are to be practiced in meaningful discourse contexts. The use of different meaningful contexts is essential, because it provides learning conditions in which the students can develop both spontaneous responses and a better understanding of the new pattern. Communicative activities in this book will provide rich contexts that help to avoid rote memorization on the part of the learner.

Language use is affected by contexts that are larger than the sentence level. One of the key characteristics of advanced learners is their ability to narrate and describe with paragraph-length connected discourse.

Sustain Students' Motivation to Communicate

In designing this book, we assume that instructional materials should be relevant, meaningful, and challenging, but not overwhelming, so that we can keep students motivated to communicate with each other. One useful technique we have adopted is to create information gaps and opinion gaps on the part of learners. We try to create the information gap by providing communicative tasks, such as getting information from other people or problem-solving. The opinion gap is created through controversial texts and discussion topics that are interesting to advanced learners.

Let the Classroom be Student-centered

Instructional materials should encourage student-centered teaching. We do not encourage teachers to spend too much class time explaining sentence by sentence. This should be avoided, especially for advanced learners. For each chapter, we provide detailed explanations and examples of the grammatical patterns and new words and phrases, as well as detailed instructions about what they are supposed to do in class. Students should study each chapter carefully by themselves before coming to the class and be prepared for class discussion. Communicative activities in this book are task-based, encourage genuine active communication, and create a meaning-centered and student-centered atmosphere. Teachers should engage students in different kinds of communicative tasks that require the use of the new vocabulary, grammatical patterns, discourse device, cultural information, etc. The teacher's role should be that of enforcing accuracy and fine-tuning, facilitating, and providing optimal learning conditions that motivate and sustain the students' desire to communicate.

The Structure of the Book

Each of the 15 chapters in this book consists of a model dialogue, a set of discussion questions, a list of new words, grammar explanation, text pattern explanation with relevant cohesive ties, and an extensive list of supplementary vocabulary that students will find useful in their required communicative performance. The last two parts are a set of exercises and activities to reinforce what they have learned from the chapter.

Both simplified and traditional characters are provided for texts, new vocabulary, patterns, exercises, and activities. A Suggested Teaching Methodology Index and Vocabulary Index are given at the end of the book. The first index starts with a well-specified communicative objective for each chapter from which one can see that the focus of the objectives is on the communication task, not the language itself. However, it does not mean that we ignore linguistic accuracy. The teaching of words and grammar is viewed as an important means (not an end) for achieving the goal of communication. After the objectives, we present some suggested procedures for teaching and learning which deal with different kinds of meaningful activities and discussion topics that the teacher can use to engage students in communication. Teaching aids and other relevant material are also suggested for the teacher's reference.

A set of audiotapes is also available from Cheng & Tsui Company.

目录
TABLE OF CONTENTS

目錄
TABLE OF CONTENTS

【第一課】

童年往事

【课文】

童年的经历

过去，我很少回忆童年时的生活。好像第一次认真地回忆还是刚进大学不久，那是由我的一位同学引起的。一天他对我说："我虽然不太了解你，但是一看你的样子，就能猜出你的家庭背景。"我听了以后很吃惊，心里想我脸上和衣服上又没有写着什么，他怎么知道我的家庭背景呢？为了确定他真有那样的能力，我就说："那你讲讲我的童年是怎样的。"他听后很坦然地说："你父亲可能是个书生，很喜欢读书，也很诚实，所以，他在你很小的时候就教育你好好读书，多学知识。同时还教育你要作诚实的人。由于你父亲的影响，你到现在还仍然认为我们每个人都应该与人为善、与书为友。"听了这位同学的一席话，我大吃一惊，因为他说的都是对的。从那以后，我常常回忆童年时的生活，并且慢慢地认识到童年的经历对一个人以后的成长的确有很大的影响。假如我的童年的经历和实际的不一样，那么，我现在是一个什么样的人呢？

讨论题：
1. 你认为什么样的童年是最美好的？为什么？
2. 童年时失去父亲或母亲对一个人的成长会有什么影响？
3. 童年时读太多书对一个人的成长有好处吗？为什么？
4. 家庭富裕对孩子的成长一定有好处吗？
5. 你小的时候跟别的孩子有什么不同？为什么？

【課文】

童年的經歷

　　過去，我很少回憶童年時的生活。好像第一次認真地回憶還是剛進大學不久，那是由我的一位同學引起的。一天他對我說："我雖然不太瞭解你，但是一看你的樣子，就能猜出你的家庭背景。"我聽了以後很吃驚，心裏想我臉上和衣服上又沒有寫着甚麼，他怎麼知道我的家庭背景呢？為了確定他真有那樣的能力，我就說："那你講講我的童年是怎樣的。"他聽後很坦然地說："你父親可能是個書生，很喜歡讀書，也很誠實，所以，他在你很小的時候就教育你好好讀書，多學知識。同時還教育你要作誠實的人。由於你父親的影響，你到現在還仍然認為我們每個人都應該與人為善、與書為友。"聽了這位同學的一席話，我大吃一驚，因為他說的都是對的。從那以後，我常常回憶童年時的生活，並且慢慢地認識到童年的經歷對一個人以後的成長的確有很大的影響。假如我童年的經歷和實際的不一樣，那麼，我現在是一個甚麼樣的人呢？

討論題：
1. 你認為甚麼樣的童年是最美好的？為甚麼？
2. 童年時失去父親或母親對一個人的成長會有甚麼影響？
3. 童年時讀太多書對一個人的成長有好處嗎？為甚麼？
4. 家庭富裕對孩子的成長一定有好處嗎？
5. 你小的時候跟別的孩子有甚麼不同？為甚麼？

【生词/生詞】

1. 童年	tóngnián	n.	childhood
2. 回忆（憶）	huíyì	v./n.	to recollect; recall
3. 好像	hǎoxiàng	v.	to seem, to appear
4. 认真（認）	rènzhēn	adj.	(to be) serious, diligent
5. 刚（剛）	gāng	adv.	just
6. 引起	yǐnqǐ	v.	to cause
7. 了解（瞭）	liǎojiě	v./n.	to understand; understanding
8. 猜出	cāichū	v.	to guess
9. 家庭	jiātíng	n.	family
10. 背景	bèijǐng	n.	background
11. 吃惊（驚）	chījīng	v.	to be surprised
12. 确定（確定）	quèdìng	v.	to make sure
13. 真	zhēn	adv.	indeed, really
14. 坦然地	tǎnránde	adv.	at ease, calmly
15. 书生（書）	shūshēng	n.	intellectual, scholar
16. 诚实（誠實）	chéngshí	adj.	(to be) honest
17. 教育	jiàoyù	v./n	to educate; education
18. 知识（識）	zhīshí	n.	knowledge
19. 影响（響）	yǐngxiǎng	n./v.	influence; to influence
20. 与人为善（與、爲）	yǔrénwéishàn	v.p.	to be kind to people
21. 与书为友（與書爲）	yǔshūwéiyǒu	v.p.	to treasure books as friends
22. 席	xí	cl.	a number of (words)
23. 慢慢地	mànmànde	adv.	slowly
24. 假如	jiǎrú	conj.	if...
25. 实际（實際）	shíjì	n./adv.	reality, fact; in fact

【句型】

一. 好像 *verb phrase* (which cannot be negated): to seem as if..., to look ...

    1.   我好像在什么地方见过您，可就是一下子想不起来。

          （我好像在甚麼地方見過您，可就是一下子想不起來。）

          "It seems as though I have seen you somewhere, but I just don't remember the place at this moment."

    2.   你好像不高兴，发生了什么事吗？

          （你好像不高興，發生了甚麼事嗎？）

          "You look unhappy. Has anything happened?"

    3.   好像他说的都是对的，而我说的都是错的。

          （好像他說的都是對的，而我說的都是錯的。）

          "It seems as if everything he said was right, but everything I said was wrong."

二. 是由...引起的 *verb phrase*: to be caused by

    1.   那次争吵是由他引起的。

          （那次爭吵是由他引起的。）

          "That fight was caused by him."

    2.   听说他们离婚是由于双方感情不合引起的。

          （聽說他們離婚是由於雙方感情不合引起的。）

          "It is said that their divorce was caused by their inability to get along."

    3.   那次事故是由什么引起的？

          （那次事故是由甚麼引起的？）

          "What caused that accident? (lit.: That accident was caused by what.)"

三. 影响 （影響） *verb/noun*: to influence; influence

    1.   由于受了一些坏同学的影响，他常常不回家。

          （由於受了一些壞同學的影響，他常常不回家。）

          "Having been influenced by some bad classmates, he often does not go home."

2. 家庭教育对每一个孩子的成长有很大的影响。

   （家庭教育對每一個孩子的成長有很大的影響。）

   "Family discipline has a great influence on every child's development."

3. 父母的一言一行都会影响到孩子。

   （父母的一言一行都會影響到孩子。）

   "Parents' every word and deed can influence their children."

四. 假如 *verb phrase*: suppose..., if...; This phrase introduces a sentence of presupposition.

1. 假如世界上沒有坏人，那该有多好。

   （假如世界上沒有壞人，那該有多好。）

   "What a nice world this would be if there were no evil people."

2. 假如他不来帮我，我一定作不完我的功课。

   （假如他不來幫我，我一定作不完我的功課。）

   "If he had not helped me, I would not have been able to finish my homework."

3. 假如他不来，你怎么办？

   （假如他不來，你怎麼辦？）

   "Suppose he did not come, what would you do?"

【语法/語法】

语文连接词/語文連接詞
(Discourse Connectors)

When we speak or write, we not only use many different sentences, but also different discourse connectors to link those sentences. This is true of Chinese, English and many other languages. As an intermediate high or advanced student, it is extremely important to learn how to use discourse connectors, because you are now at the stage of learning how to speak and write coherent paragraphs, not just sentences. In this lesson, we will discuss three of the most commonly used discourse connectors in Chinese. They are: 而且,並且 "and, but also"; 但是/可是 "but, however"; 或(者) "or".

First, let us look at 而且/並且. Both of these connectors can be interpreted as "and, but also" and connect two sentences which are most likely to express foregrounding or sequential situation. In other words, the sentence following the connector either provides further information to the statement made in the previous sentence, or it provides information parallel to the immediately preceding sentence. For instance:

1. 一年沒见，你个子长高了，身体长壮了，而且性格也好像更开朗了。
   （一年沒見，你個子長高了，身體長壯了，而且性格也好像更開朗了。）
   "I haven't seen you for a year. You are taller, stronger, and your personality also seems more open."

2. 我觉得童年的生活很有意思，那时候想做什么做什么，并且不必担心吃饭的问题。
   （我覺得童年的生活很有意思，那時候想做甚麼做甚麼，並且不必擔心吃飯的問題。）
   "I feel that the childhood experience is very interesting: one can do whatever s/he wants to do, without worrying about the problem of putting food on the table."

3. 他不但（不仅）喜欢现代音乐，而且（并且）喜欢古典音乐。

（他不但（不僅）喜歡現代音樂，而且（並且）喜歡古典音樂。）
"He not only likes modern music, but also classical music."

而且 and 並且 are often used with 不但/不僅: the latter occurs in the first sentence, and the former occurs in the second sentence, as shown in 3. 且 can sometimes be omitted. However, students should be aware that when 而 is used by itself, it can express many different meanings in addition to what we have just discussed.

As for 但是 and 可是, they can be interpreted as "but, however", and are quite different from the two just discussed. 但是/可是 are primarily used to connect two contrasting sentences. For example:

4. 我们已经培养了不少人才，但是还不能满足实际需要。
   （我們已經培養了不少人才，但是還不能滿足實際需要。）
   "We have already trained many people; but/however, the practical needs still cannot be met."

5. 美国菜好是好，可是我不喜欢。
   （美國菜好是好，可是我不喜歡。）
   "American food is good, but I don't like it."

但是/可是 often occurs in conjunction with 雖然/盡管 in two consecutive sentences: 雖然/盡管 is used in the first sentence, and 但是/可是 used in the second sentence. The first sentence expresses concession, like the English conjunction "(al)though" in 6.

6. 虽然美国菜好吃，但是我从来不做，因为太麻烦。
   （雖然美國菜好吃，但是我從來不做，因為太麻煩。）
   "Although American food is good, I never cook it because it takes too much time."

The 是 in 但是/可是 can be omitted. When, 但/可 is used by itself, it still expresses the above meaning with certain stylistic differences. Furthermore, it can also express some other meanings. For instance, 可 can be interpreted as "can/could". Another connector which is similar to 但是/可是 in its discourse function is 然而. The difference between them is that the latter is more formal in style.

Finally, 或(者), different from both previous types of connectors, is commonly used to express alternation between two sentences, as illustrated in 7 and 8:

7. 星期天我沒事，你可以到我家来，或者我到你家去。
   （星期天我沒事，你可以到我家來，或者我到你家去。）

   "I don't have anything to do on Sunday. You can either come to my house, or I could go to your house."

8. 或者你同意，或者你反对，总得表示个态度。
   （或者你同意，或者你反對，總得表示個態度。）

   "You must tell us your opinion: you can either agree or disagree."

Notice that 或者 can also be used in two consecutive sentences, and is equivalent to the English "either ... or..." as shown in (8). Sometimes 或 can be used by itself and retain the same function as 或者.

To summarize, we have seen that the three discourse connectors have quite different functions in discourse. 而且/並且 connect sequential situations, 但是/可是 connect contrastive situations, and 或(者) connects two alternative situations. The similarity among these three connectors is that all three types can have another connector in the immediately preceding sentences to strengthen their semantic meaning. This is a unique characteristic of Chinese discourse connectors and should be drawn to the students' attention in their study of Chinese grammar.

【补充词汇/補充詞彙】

辞类：儿童教育 〔辭類：兒童教育〕 (Child Education)

活泼 （潑）	huópō	adj.	(to be) lively
耐心	nàixīn	adj./n.	(to be) patient; patience
大胆 （膽）	dàdǎn	adj.	(to be) bold, daring
积极 （積極）	jījí	adj.	(to be) active/enthusiastic
乐观 （樂觀）	lèguān	adj.	(to be) optimistic
悲观 （觀）	bēiguān	adj.	(to be) pessimistic
用功	yònggōng	adj.	(to be) hardworking
害羞	hàixiū	adj.	(to be) shy
勇敢	yǒnggǎn	adj.	(to be) brave
勤奋 （奮）	qínfèn	adj.	(to be) hardworking
仔细 （細）	zǐxì	adj.	(to be) careful
训练 （訓練）	xùnliàn	v./n.	to train; training
激发 （發）	jīfā	v.	to stimulate
鼓励 （勵）	gǔlì	v./n.	to encourage; encouragement
培养 （養）	péiyǎng	v.	to cultivate, to bring up
注意	zhùyì	v.	to pay attention
奖励 （獎勵）	jiǎnglì	v./n.	to encourage by a bonus; reward
探讨 （討）	tàntǎo	v.	to explore
表演	biǎoyǎn	v./n.	to perform; performance
善于 （於）	shànyú	v.	to be good at
重视 （視）	zhòngshì	v.	to emphasize
基本功	jīběngōng	n.	basics, foundation
方法	fāngfǎ	n.	way, method
习惯 （習慣）	xíguàn	n./v.	custom, habit; to be used to
兴趣 （興）	xìngqù	n.	interest
智慧	zhìhuì	n.	talent

【练习】

一. 完成句子：

1. 由于受父母的影响，我现在 _____。

2. 过去，他学习很认真，可是 _____。

3. 假如我有一百万美元的话， _____。

4. 虽然他常常教育孩子要与人为善 _____。

5. 他好像受了坏人的影响，因为他常常 _____。

6. 这家店里的衣服我都_____但是_____。

7. 他做的中国菜很好，但是 _____。

二. 造句：

1. 对……有……影响

2. 虽然……但是……

3. 是由……引起的……

4. 假如......

5. 并且

三. 选词填空：

　　　　但是　与书为友　和　教育　而且　影响

孩子很小的时候父母就应该 ＿＿＿＿＿＿ 他们 ＿＿＿＿＿＿、与人为善，因为童年的教育对孩子的成长有很大的 ＿＿＿＿＿＿ 。另外，父母也要培养孩子学习的兴趣 ＿＿＿＿＿＿ 独立思考的能力。兴趣是求知的动力。 ＿＿＿＿＿＿ 只有学习的兴趣还不够，孩子很小的时候就要学会独立思考， ＿＿＿＿＿＿ 要学会怎么样解决问题。

四. 作文：你小的时候跟别的孩子有什么不同？举例说明.
(50-100字) Be prepared to talk about this in class.

【練習】

一. 完成句子：

1. 由於受父母的影響，我現在 _____。

2. 過去，他學習很認真，可是 _____。

3. 假如我有一百萬美元的話，_____。

4. 雖然他常常教育孩子要與人為善 _____。

5. 他好像受了壞人的影響，因為他常常 _____。

6. 這家店裡的衣服我都_____但是_____。

7. 他做的中國菜很好，但是_____。

二. 造句：

1. 對......有......影響

2. 雖然......但是......

3. 是由......引起的......

4. 假如......

5. 並且

三. 選詞填空：

　　　但是　與書為友　和　教育　而且　影響

孩子很小的時候父母就應該 _____ 他們 _____、與人為善，因為童年的教育對孩子的成長有很大的 _____ 。另外，父母也要培養孩子學習的興趣 _____ 獨立思考的能力。興趣是求知的動力。 _____ 只有學習的興趣還不夠，孩子很小的時候就要學會獨立思考， _____ 要學會怎麼樣解決問題。

四. 作文：你小的時候跟別的孩子有甚麼不同？舉例說明.
(50-100字) Be prepared to talk about this in class.

【衍生活动】

请写完下面"我家的故事"中的句子，并在课堂上讲给同学听。

1. 我家有 _____ 人。

2. 爸爸教育我们要 _____ ，而且 _____ 。

3. 我小的时候喜欢和弟弟吵架，我们之间的问题常常是由 _____ 引起的。

4. 妈妈年轻的时候念了大学，但是 _____ 。

5. 姐姐不但喜欢 _____ 也喜欢 _____ ，

   并且 _____ 。

6. 哥哥是我的好朋友，他的 _____ 对我有很大的影响，可是

   _____ 。

7. 假如我的家 _____ ，我们的情况会比现在好得多。

8. 虽然 _____ 但是 _____ 。

9. 我爱我的家人，并且 _____ 。

10. 最后， _____ 。

【衍生活動】

請寫完下面 "我家的故事" 中的句子，並在課堂上講給同學聽。

1. 我家有 _____人。

2. 爸爸教育我們要 _____，而且 _____。

3. 我小的時候喜歡和弟弟吵架，我們之間的問題常常是由 _____ 引起的。

4. 媽媽年輕的時候唸了大學，但是 _____。

5. 姐姐不但喜歡 _____ 也喜歡 _____，

   並且 _____。

6. 哥哥是我的好朋友，他的 _____對我有很大的影響，

   可是 _____。

7. 假如我的家_____，我們的情況會比現在好得多。

8. 雖然 _____ 但是 _____。

9. 我愛我的家人，並且 _____。

10. 最後，_____。

【第二课】

描述一个人

【课文】

描述一个人

甲： 你认为邓小平这个人怎么样？

乙： 我觉得他很伟大。他的一生那么不平凡，为中国做了很多了不起的事。我非常敬佩他。

丙： 依我看，邓小平是个自私自利、心狠手辣的独裁者。

乙： 你根据什么说他自私自利、心狠手辣？

丙： 给你举个最简单的例子，一九八九年天安门事件，邓小平为了自己的利益，不仅命令军队枪杀了很多学生，而且还撤消了赵紫阳的总书记职务。你说他是不是自私自利、心狠手辣？

乙： 他那样做也许有不得已的苦衷。

甲： 就外表而言，他看上去很冷静，也很诚实。

丙： 没那么回事！他长了一脸毒相。

乙： 你们的看法，我都不同意。虽然他长得不那么帅，但是还算大方，能看得过去。我认为用『平凡』而『伟大』这两个词来形容邓小平这个人是最合适的。

讨论题：
1. 你认为邓小平这个人怎么样？
2. 你最喜欢的人是什么样的？
3. 你最讨厌的人是什么样的？

【課文】

描述一個人

甲： 你認為鄧小平這個人怎麼樣？

乙： 我覺得他很偉大。他的一生那麼不平凡，為中國做了很多了不起的事。我非常敬佩他。

丙： 依我看，鄧小平是個自私自利、心狠手辣的獨裁者。

乙： 你根據甚麼說他自私自利、心狠手辣？

丙： 給你舉個最簡單的例子，一九八九年天安門事件，鄧小平為了自己的利益不僅命令軍隊槍殺了很多學生，而且還撤消了趙紫陽的總書記職務。你說他是不是自私自利、心狠手辣？

乙： 他那樣做也許有不得已的苦衷。

甲： 就外表而言，他看上去很冷靜，也很誠實。

丙： 沒那麼回事！他長了一臉毒相。

乙： 你們的看法，我都不同意。雖然他長得不那麼帥，但是還算大方，能看得過去。我認為用『平凡』而『偉大』這兩個詞來形容鄧小平這個人是最合適的。

討論題：
1. 你認為鄧小平這個人怎麼樣？
2. 你最喜歡的人是甚麼樣的？
3. 你最討厭的人是甚麼樣的？

【生词/生詞】

1. 描述	miáoshù	v./n.	to describe; description
2. 认为（認爲）	rènwéi	v.	to believe, to think
3. 觉得（覺）	juéde	v.	to feel
4. 伟大（偉）	wěidà	adj.	(to be) great
5. 一生	yìshēng	n.	(whole) life
6. 平凡	píngfán	adj.	(to be) ordinary
7. 了不起	liǎobùqǐ	v.p.	to be extraordinary
8. 敬佩	jìngpèi	v.	to respect, to admire
9. 利益	lìyì	n.	benefit
10. 自私自利	zìsīzìlì	adj.p.	(to be) selfish
11. 心狠手辣	xīnhěnshǒulà	adj.p.	(to be) wicked
12. 独裁者（獨）	dúcáizhě	n.	dictator
13. 根据（據）	gēnjù	conj./n.	according to; grounds
14. 举（舉）	jǔ	v.	to give (an example)
15. 例子	lìzi	n.	example
16. 事件	shìjiàn	n.	event, incident
17. 命令	mìnglìng	n./v.	command; to command
18. 枪杀（槍殺）	qiāngshā	v.	to kill (with guns)
19. 撤消	chèxiāo	v.	to dismiss, to revoke
20. 总理（總）	zǒnglǐ	n.	premier
21. 职务（職務）	zhíwù	n.	position
22. 苦衷	kǔzhōng	n.	something difficult to discuss
23. 冷静	lěngjìng	adj.	(to be) calm
24. 毒	dú	adj.	(to be) merciless
25. 帅（帥）	shuài	adj.	(to be) good-looking (male)
26. 大方	dàfāng	adj.	(to be) well-poised

【句型】

一. 依我看 *adverbial phrase*: to me...; in my opinion. This phrase is placed at the beginning of a sentence or a group of sentences to initiate an opinion.

    1. 依我看，他长得并不怎么样。

    （依我看，他長得並不怎麼樣。）

    "To me, he looks quite ordinary."

    2. 依我看，人的长相并不重要，重要的是他诚实不诚实。

    （依我看，人的長相並不重要，重要的是他誠實不誠實。）

    "In my opinion, one's appearance is not important; what is important is whether he is honest or not."

    3. 依我看，他很古怪，可是很善良，比方说他总是乐于助人。

    （依我看，他很古怪，可是很善良，比方説他總是樂於助人。）

    "To me, he is very eccentric; however, he is kindhearted. For instance, he always likes to help others."

二. 看上去 *verb phrase* (which cannot be negated): to seem...; to look like...

    1. 他看上去长得不错。

    （他看上去長得不錯。）

    "He seems to have a pretty nice appearance."

    2. 看上去他不像个生病的人。

    （看上去他不像個生病的人。）

    "He does not look like a sick person."

    3. 他看上去只有四十多岁，谁知道他孙子已经上小学了。

    （他看上去只有四十多歲，誰知道他孫子已經上小學了。）

    "From his appearance, he seems only forty years old. Who would know his grandson is already in elementary school?!"

三. 有（没）那么回事/有（沒）那麼回事 *verb phrase*: There is (no) such a thing! That is (not) right! This phrase helps formulate a structure of strong (dis)agreement.

1. 你说他不喜欢电影，根本没那么回事，我每次看电影都能碰见他。

   （你説他不喜歡電影，根本沒那麼回事，我每次看電影都能碰見他。）

   "You said he did not like movies. This can't be true. I see him every

   time I go to a movie."

2. 有的学生觉得老师不公平，实际上并不是那么回事。

   （有的學生覺得老師不公平，實際上並不是那麼回事。）

   "Some students do not think that the teacher is fair. In reality, this cannot

   be true."

3. 我记得有那么回事，可是我不感兴趣。

   （我記得有那麼回事，可是我不感興趣。）

   "I remember that there was something like that, but I was not interested

   in it."

四. 不得已 *adjective phrase*: no other choice; to have to... Structurally, this phrase
occurs in 1)...的时候 ...的办法，2) Subject + 是+不得已，3) 不得已 + Sentence.

1. 他从来不逃课，即使是不得已的时候他也会事先跟老师请假。

   （他從來不逃課，即使是不得已的時候他也會事先跟老師請假。）

   "He has never cut classes. Even when he has to miss one, he always tells

   the teacher in advance."

2. 他那样作完全是不得已。

   （他那樣作完全是不得已。）

   "He did that only because there was no other choice."

3. 礼堂太小，不得已，很多人只好站在外边听讲演。

   （禮堂太小，不得已，很多人只好站在外邊聽講演。）

   "The auditorium is too small; many people have to stand outside listening

   to the speech."

五. 长了一脸（副）...相/長了一臉（副）...相 *verb phrase*: to look (a certain
way)

1. 他长了一副老实相。

   （他長了一副老實相。）

   "He looks honest."

2. 我有一个同学，长了一副可怜相。

（我有一個同學，長了一副可憐相。）

"I have a classmate who looks pitiable."

3. 那个人长了一脸奸相。

（那個人長了一臉奸相。）

"That person looks evil."

六. 还算/還算 *verb phrase*: to be still counted/considered as

1. 我朋友的功课还算不错。

（我朋友的功課還算不錯。）

"My friend's grades can be considered good."

2. 这本书还算有用。

（這本書還算有用。）

"This book is still considered useful."

3. 他还算够朋友。

（他還算夠朋友。）

"He still can be counted as a friend."

七. ...看得过去。/...看得過去。 *verb phrase*: to look okay. This phrase expresses the opinion that, although it is not great, it looks okay. There are other similar phrases such as ...听得过去, ...说得过去。 To negate, 不 is used to replace 得.

1. 他的长相看得过去。

（他的長相看得過去。）

"He looks okay."

2. 这件衣服不是很好看，可是还算看得过去。

（這件衣服不是很好看，可是還算看得過去。）

"These clothes are not very pretty, but they are still okay."

3. 这话也说得过去。

（這話也說得過去。）

"These words were not overstated (i.e., They are fine)."

【语法/語法】

语序的变换/語序的變換
(Alternative Word Orders)

Chinese normally has SVO (subject-verb-object) order, but when a speaker wants to emphasize an object (often mentioned in preceding discourse) or contrast the object with something else, the object is often moved to the preverbal position, as in this sentence from the text: 你们的看法，我都不同意。 （你們的看法，我都不同意。） "Your opinions, I disagree." Here the object is emphasized. Following are a few more examples:

1. 这些书，我都看过了。 （這些書，我都看過了。）

   "These books are some that I have already read."

2. 我们连录音机都买不到。 （我們連錄音機都買不到。）

   "We could not even find a tape recorder."

3. 现在电视很好买，可是好的电视买不到。

   （現在電視很好買，可是好的電視買不到。）

   "Now it is easy to buy a TV; however, good ones are hard to get."

All of the objects in the three preceding sentences are emphasized or contrasted with other elements. However, the structures of the three sentences are somewhat different: Sentence 1 has OSV word order. Sentence 2 has SOV order with the emphatic word 连/連 proceding the object. Sentence 3 has OV order with the subject omitted*. This is to say that if we want to emphasize an object, we could use all three types of word order.

Another cue that is often used to signal the emphasis of objects is the word 都, as shown in sentence 1, and in fact it is almost always the case that the empatic words 连/連 or 甚至 are used together with 都, as shown in Sentence 2.

*The terms "subject" and "object" are used here purely for the convenience of students. They do not indicate any theoretical claim of the authors of this book.

【补充词汇/補充詞彙】

描述人的生词(Each of the following words can be used as an adjective or a stative verb):

酷	kù	(to be) cool (e.g. people)
精	jīng	(to be) smart, clever
蠢	chǔn	(to be) stupid
直	zhí	(to be) straightforward
野	yě	(to be) wild
狠	hěn	(to be) ruthless
贪 (貪)	tān	(to be) greedy
娇 (嬌)	jiāo	(to be) squeamish
乐观 (樂觀)	lèguān	(to be) optimistic
悲观 (觀)	bēiguān	(to be) pessimistic
虚伪 (偽)	xūwěi	(to be) hypocritical
小气 (氣)	xiǎoqì	(to be) stingy
俗气 (氣)	súqì	(to be) vulgar
高雅	gāoyǎ	(to be) elegant
仔细 (細)	zǐxì	(to be) careful
粗心	cūxīn	(to be) careless
敏感	mǐngǎn	(to be) sensitive
迟钝 (遲鈍)	chídùn	(to be) slow in response
性感	xìnggǎn	(to be) sexy
冷静	lěngjìng	(to be) calm
骄傲 (驕)	jiāo'ào	(to be) arrogant
谦虚 (謙)	qiānxū	(to be) modest
幽默	yōumò	(to be) humorous
滑稽	huájī	(to be) funny
自卑	zìbēi	(to feel onself) inferior

同情	tóngqíng	(to be) sympathetic
体谅 (體諒)	tǐliàng	(to be) considerate
体贴 (體貼)	tǐtiē	(to be) considerate
多情	duōqíng	(to be) full of affection
幼稚	yòuzhì	(to be) childish
自负 (負)	zìfù	(to be) arrogant
唯利是图 (圖)	wéilìshìtú	only intent on profit
妄自尊大	wàngzìzūndà	(to be) arrogant
热情洋溢 (熱)	rèqíngyángyì	(to be) enthusiastic
冷若冰霜	lěngruòbīngshuāng	(to be) cold
沉默寡言	chénmòguǎyán	(to be) silent
油腔滑调 (調)	yóuqiānghuádiào	(to be) glib
贪得无厌 (貪、厭)	tāndéwúyàn	(to be) greedy
安分守己	ānfènshǒujǐ	to know one's place
自作聪明 (聰)	zìzuòcōngmíng	to think oneself clever
自以为是 (爲)	zìyǐwéishì	(to be) opinionated

【练习】

一. 完成句子：

1. 人们都说他是一个自私自利的人，依我看＿＿＿＿＿＿＿＿＿＿＿＿＿＿＿＿＿。

2. 他看上去 ＿＿＿＿＿＿＿＿＿＿＿＿＿＿＿＿＿＿＿＿＿＿＿＿＿＿＿。

3. ＿＿＿＿＿＿＿＿＿＿＿＿＿＿＿＿＿＿＿＿＿＿＿还看得过去。

4. 他一生都 ＿＿＿＿＿＿＿＿＿＿＿＿＿＿＿＿＿＿＿＿＿＿＿＿＿＿＿。

5. 不得已的时候，他连＿＿＿＿＿＿＿＿＿＿＿＿＿＿＿＿＿＿＿＿＿＿。

二. 造句：

1. 了不起

2. 沒那么回事

3. 不得已

4. 根据

5. 举个例子

三. 用下面的词填空(Fill in the blanks using the words given):

长相　看上去　有人　对　个子　胖　善良　看

　　孟子是中国历史上一个很有名的人。过去和现在有很多人研究他的文章，可是很少人研究过他的_____。有人说他一定很有学问，_____说他可能是个善良的人，还有人说他可能_____学生很严厉。从他的学生的文章看，孟子的_____可能很高，身体有一点儿_____，长得也不帅，但是他的学问很高。他的思想对后人的影响很大，特别是在人的本性和道德方面。按照孟子的说法，人生下来的时候都是_____的，但是长大的时候，由于受到不好的教导和影响，有些人就慢慢地变坏了。此外，孟子还认为我们看一个人不能只看他的长相，而不_____他的行为。他的这些话已成为人们生活中的格言。

四. 翻译：

1. Confucius was not only a well-known educator, but also the greatest thinker in history. His thought has had great influence on Chinese culture. Many people have done research on Confucius.

2. Sometimes she is friendly; sometimes she is as cold as ice. Many people say that she is eccentric, but in my opinion, she is a very kindhearted person. For instance, she is always ready to help other people.

五. 短文：描写一个你最喜欢或者最厌恶的人 〔150字以上〕。You should use the following text structures in your composition.

    1. Time-order structure for describing a person:

＿＿＿＿出生在＿＿＿＿＿＿＿＿＿＿＿＿＿＿＿ 那时侯 ＿＿＿＿＿＿＿＿＿＿＿＿＿＿＿＿。

他曾＿＿＿＿＿＿＿＿＿＿＿＿＿＿＿＿＿＿ 后来 ＿＿＿＿＿＿＿＿＿＿＿＿＿＿＿＿＿。

    2. Argumentation Structure:

在我看来＿＿＿＿＿＿＿＿＿＿＿＿＿＿＿＿＿＿＿ 是个 ＿＿＿＿＿＿＿＿＿＿＿＿＿＿＿。

给你举个例子，他……

【練習】

一. 完成句子：

1. 人們都説他是一個自私自利的人，依我看＿＿＿＿＿＿＿＿＿＿＿＿＿＿＿＿＿＿＿。

2. 他看上去 ＿＿＿＿＿＿＿＿＿＿＿＿＿＿＿＿＿＿＿＿＿＿＿＿＿＿。

3. ＿＿＿＿＿＿＿＿＿＿＿＿＿＿＿＿＿＿＿＿＿還看得過去。

4. 他一生都 ＿＿＿＿＿＿＿＿＿＿＿＿＿＿＿＿＿＿＿＿＿＿＿＿＿。

5. 不得已的時候，他連＿＿＿＿＿＿＿＿＿＿＿＿＿＿＿＿＿＿＿＿＿＿。

二. 造句：

1. 了不起

2. 沒那麼回事

3. 不得已

4. 根據

5. 舉個例子

三. 用下面的詞填空(Fill in the blanks using the words given):

長相　看上去　有人　對　個子　胖　善良　看

　　孟子是中國歷史上一個很有名的人。過去和現在有很多人研究他的文章，可是很少人研究過他的 _____。有人說他一定很有學問，_____ 說他可能是個善良的人，還有人說他可能 _____ 學生很嚴厲。從他的學生的文章看，孟子的 _____ 可能不高，身體有一點兒 _____，長得也不帥，但是他的學問很高。他的思想對後人的影響很大，特別是在人的本性和道德方面。按照孟子的說法，人生下來的時候都是 _____ 的，但是長大的時候，由於受到不好的教導和影響，有些人就慢慢地變壞了。此外，孟子還認為我們看一個人不能只看他的長相，而不 _____ 他的行為。他的這些話已成為人們生活中的格言。

四. 翻譯：

1. Confucius was not only a well-known educator, but also the greatest thinker in history. His thought has had great influence on Chinese culture. Many people have done research on Confucius.

2. Sometimes she is friendly; sometimes she is as cold as ice. Many people say that she is eccentric, but in my opinion, she is a very kindhearted person. For instance she is always ready to help other people.

五. 短文：描寫一個你最喜歡或者最厭惡的人（150字以上）。You should use the following text structures in your composition.

1. Time-order structure for describing a person:

＿＿＿ 出生在＿＿＿＿＿＿＿＿＿＿＿＿＿＿ 那時侯 ＿＿＿＿＿＿＿＿＿＿＿＿＿。

他曾＿＿＿＿＿＿＿＿＿＿＿＿＿＿，後來 ＿＿＿＿＿＿＿＿＿＿＿＿＿＿＿。

2. Argumentation Structure:

在我看來＿＿＿＿＿＿＿＿＿＿＿＿＿＿是個 ＿＿＿＿＿＿＿＿＿＿＿＿＿＿。

給你舉個例子， 他......

【衍生活动】

填写履历

请将下列求职时所用的表格、问题写好，带到课堂上与同学、老师讨论。

I. 填写表格：

1. 姓名 ＿＿＿＿＿＿
2. 出生日期 ＿＿＿＿＿＿
3. 身分证号码 ＿＿＿＿＿＿
4. 籍贯 ＿＿＿＿＿＿
5. 住址 ＿＿＿＿＿＿
6. 电话号码 ＿＿＿＿＿＿
7. 驾照号码 ＿＿＿＿＿＿
8. 传真机号码 ＿＿＿＿＿＿
9. 婚姻状况 ＿＿＿＿＿＿
10. 经历 ＿＿＿＿＿＿
11. 服务单位 ＿＿＿＿＿＿
12. 现职 ＿＿＿＿＿＿
13. 年薪 ＿＿＿＿＿＿
14. 配偶姓名 ＿＿＿＿＿＿
15. 紧急联络人 ＿＿＿＿＿＿
16. 血型 ＿＿＿＿＿＿
17. 嗜好 ＿＿＿＿＿＿
18. 专长 ＿＿＿＿＿＿
19. 身高 ＿＿＿＿＿＿
20. 体重 ＿＿＿＿＿＿
21. 最高学历 ＿＿＿＿＿＿
22. 主修 ＿＿＿＿＿＿
23. 副修 ＿＿＿＿＿＿
24. 工作时间 ＿＿＿＿＿＿
25. 希望待遇 ＿＿＿＿＿＿
26. 离职原因 ＿＿＿＿＿＿

II. 讨论题：

1. 就本表格来看，哪些项目(items)和美国常用的表格项目不同？
2. 从表格中可看出中国人和西方人的"隐私"(privacy)范围有何不同？
3. 写自传应注意哪些事情？有什么禁忌？

【衍生活動】

填寫履歷

請將下列求職時所用的表格、問題寫好，帶到課堂上與同學、老師討論。

I. 填寫表格：

name	1. 姓名 _____	DOB	2. 出生日期 _____
id #	3. 身分證號碼 _____	birth place	4. 籍貫 _____
address	5. 住址 _____	tele	6. 電話號碼 _____
passport	7. 駕照號碼 _____	fax	8. 傳真機號碼 _____
marital	9. 婚姻狀況 _____	exp.	10. 經歷 _____
	11. 服務單位 _____	present job	12. 現職 _____
	13. 年薪 _____		14. 配偶姓名 _____
emerg.cont	15. 緊急聯絡人 _____	blood	16. 血型 _____
habit	17. 嗜好 _____	specialty	18. 專長 _____
height	19. 身高 _____	weight	20. 體重 _____
education	21. 最高學歷 _____	major	22. 主修 _____
minor	23. 副修 _____	times of employment	24. 工作時間 _____
	25. 希望待遇 _____	reason why left job	26. 離職原因 _____

II. 討論題：

1. 就本表格來看，哪些項目(items)和美國常用的表格項目不同？
2. 從表格中可看出中國人和西方人的 "隱私" (privacy)範圍有何不同？
3. 寫自傳應注意哪些事情？有甚麼禁忌？

american resumes
benefits american

【第三課】

推銷高手

【课文】

推销高手

（推销员与顾客）

甲： 您好！我是MCI电话公司。最近...

乙： 又是电话公司的推销员，一会儿是AT&T，一会儿是SPRINT，现在是MCI. 对不起，我现在很忙，没有时间跟你讲话。

甲： 噢，我是想告诉您一下我们公司为了方便顾客新增设了一项业务。这项业务...

乙： 我跟你说过我很忙没有时间跟你说话。再见。（挂了电话）

（过了一分钟）

甲： 对不起，还是我，MCI电话公司。刚才我没有把话说清楚，我知道您很忙，所以我只想跟您说一句话。

乙： 好吧，好吧。（显得不耐烦的样子）

甲： 您如果现在往中国打电话，每分钟只花四十九分，这是有史以来最低的价格。

乙： 真的吗？还是跟我开玩笑？

甲： 是真的，这个消息您也可以在各个大报纸上看到。顺便问一下，您现在往中国打电话每分钟要多少钱？

乙： 我也不太清楚，大概要一、两美元，你说每分钟四十九分，那么我什么时候打都是这个价吗？

甲： 这是周末的价格，平日也很便宜，每分钟不到一美元，不仅如此，如果您在九月三十日之前参加我们电话公司的话，您还可以得到六十美元的奖券。

乙： 奖券对我来说没有什么吸引力，因为要是我选择别的电话公司，也可以得到奖券。

甲： 但是任何一家公司都没有我们给得多。

乙： 不管怎麽说，你们这项服务听起来很有意思，让我想想，然后给你打电话，因为我得从另外一家公司转到你们公司。

甲： 您要是愿意，我现在就可以给您转。而且是免费的。这样的服务，您在别的公司是很难享受到的。

乙： 嗯…，那你就干脆给我转吧！可别忘了给我寄那六十元的奖券。

甲： 不会忘的，谢谢您选择MCI电话公司。

乙： 再见！

讨论题：
1. 如果你是一个电话公司的推销员，怎么说服顾客选择你的电话公司？
2. 什么样的衣服广告比较好？为什么？
3. 你认为广告上一定要有漂亮的姑娘吗？为什么？
4. 你认为在推销产品的时候，什么样的语言最有效？
5. 你是一个顾客，在选择一个产品的时候最注意的是什么？
6. 你买哪些商品的时候会受广告影响，为什么？
7. 有人以为商业广告充满谎言，你认为呢？

【課文】

推銷高手

（推銷員與顧客）

甲： 您好！我是MCI電話公司。最近…

乙： 又是電話公司的推銷員，一會兒是AT&T，一會兒是SPRINT，現在是MCI. 對不起，我現在很忙，沒有時間跟你講話。

甲： 噢，我是想告訴您一下我們公司為了方便顧客新增設了一項業務。這項業務…

乙： 我跟你說過我很忙沒有時間跟你說話。再見。（掛了電話）

（過了一分鐘）

甲： 對不起，還是我，MCI電話公司。剛才我沒有把話說清楚，我知道您很忙，所以我只想跟您說一句話。

乙： 好吧，好吧。（顯得不耐煩的樣子）

甲： 您如果現在往中國打電話，每分鐘只花四十九分，這是有史以來最低的價格。

乙： 真的嗎？還是跟我開玩笑？

甲： 是真的，這個消息您也可以在各個大報紙上看到。順便問一下，您現在往中國打電話每分鐘要多少錢？

乙： 我也不太清楚，大概要一、兩美元，你說每分鐘四十九分，那麼我甚麼時候打都是這個價嗎？

甲： 這是週末的價格，平日也很便宜，每分鐘不到一美元，不僅如此，如果您在九月三十日之前參加我們電話公司的話，您還可以得到六十美元的獎券。

乙： 獎券對我來說沒有甚麼吸引力，因為要是我選擇別的電話公司，也可以得到獎券。

甲： 但是任何一家公司都沒有我們給得多。

乙： 不管怎麼說，你們這項服務聽起來很有意思，讓我想想，然後給你打電話，因為我得從另外一家公司轉到你們公司。

甲： 您要是願意，我現在就可以給您轉。而且是免費的。這樣的服務，您在別的公司是很難享受到的。

乙： 嗯…，那你就乾脆給我轉吧！可別忘了給我寄那六十元的獎券。

甲： 不會忘的，謝謝您選擇MCI電話公司。

乙： 再見！

討論問題：
   1. 如果你是一個電話公司的推銷員，怎麼說服顧客選擇你的電話公司？
   2. 甚麼樣的衣服廣告比較好？為甚麼？
   3. 你認為廣告上一定要有漂亮的姑娘嗎？為甚麼？
   4. 你認為在推銷產品的時候，甚麼樣的語言最有效？
   5. 你是一個顧客，在選擇一個產品的時候最注意的是甚麼？
   6. 你買哪些商品的時候會受廣告影響，為甚麼？
   7. 有人以為商業廣告充滿謊言，你認為呢？

【生词/生詞】

1. 推销（銷）	tuīxiāo	v.	to sell
2. 高手	gāoshǒu	n.	master
3. 推销员（銷員）	tuīxiāoyuán	n.	salesperson
4. 顾客（顧）	gùkè	n.	customer
5. 方便	fāngbiàn	v./n.	to be convenient; convenience
6. 项（項）	xiàng	cl.	measure word
7. 业务（業務）	yèwù	n.	service
8. 挂（掛）	guà	v.	to hang
9. 有史以来（來）	yǒushǐyǐlái	adv.p.	since the beginning of history
10. 不耐烦（煩）	búnàifán	v.p.	to be impatient
11. 价格（價）	jiàgé	n.	price
12. 顺便（順）	shùnbiàn	adv.	in passing
13. 不到	búdào	v.p.	to be less than
14. 不仅如此（僅）	bùjǐnrúcǐ	adv.p.	not only that
15. 参加（參）	cānjiā	v.	to participate in, to join
16. 选择（選擇）	xuǎnzé	v./n.	to choose; choice
17. 奖券（獎）	jiǎngquàn	n.	bonus certificate
18. 吸引	xīyǐn	v.	to attract
19. 吸引力	xīyǐnlì	n.	attraction, attractability
20. 转（轉）	zhuǎn	v.	to switch, to turn
21. 免费（費）	miǎnfèi	adj./adv.	free of charge
22. 享受	xiǎngshòu	v./n.	to enjoy; enjoyment
23. 干脆（乾）	gāncuì	adv./adj.	straightforwardly; (to be) straightforward
24. 广告（廣）	guǎnggào	n.	advertisement
25. 说服（說）	shuōfú	v.	to persuade
26. 产品（產）	chǎnpǐn	n.	product
27. 有效	yǒuxiào	v.p.	to be effective

28. 商业（業）	shāngyè	n.	commerce
29. 谎言（謊）	huǎngyán	n.	lie

【句型】

一. 一会儿/一會兒…, 一会儿/一會兒 … *adverbial phrase*: now… now…, one moment… one moment…

    1. 这个人怎么一会儿哭，一会儿笑？

      （這個人怎麼一會兒哭，一會兒笑？）

  "Why is this person crying one moment and laughing the next."

    2. 他们一会儿说来，一会儿又说不来了。

      （他們一會兒說來，一會兒又說不來了。）

  "Just now they said they were coming, now they say they are not."

    3. 我在家一会儿看孩子，一会儿做饭。没有闲着的时候。

      （我在家一會兒看孩子，一會兒做飯。沒有閒著的時候。）

  "At home, I never have free time: one moment I am taking care of the child, the next moment I am cooking."

二. 显…（样子）/顯…（樣子）*verb phrase*: to appear

    1. 他显得很有钱的样子，实际上他很穷。

      （他顯得很有錢的樣子，實際上他很窮。）

  "He appears to have a lot of money; but in reality he is very poor."

    2. 每次讲到鬼的故事，他都显出很害怕的样子。

      （每次講到鬼的故事，他都顯出很害怕的樣子。）

  "Whenever he hears a ghost story, he appears scared."

3. 那个学生回答问题的时候，总是显得很紧张。

（那個學生回答問題的時候，總是顯得很緊張。）

"When answering questions, that student always appears very nervous."

三. 有史以来 *adverbial phrase*: in the history, ever

1. 有史以来，这是他第一次向我道歉。

（有史以來，這是他第一次向我道歉。）

"This is the first time that he ever apologized to me."

2. 这是有史以来最好的一本中文书。

（這是有史以來最好的一本中文書。）

"This is the best Chinese book ever written."

3. 这是有史以来没有过的事。

（這是有史以來沒有過的事。）

"This kind of thing has never happened before."

四. 不仅如此/不僅如此 *adverbial phrase*: not only this; in addition to this

1. 他说他不喜欢我，不仅如此，他还拒绝跟我说话。

（他說他不喜歡我，不僅如此，他還拒絕跟我說話。）

"He said he did not like me. In addition to that, he refused to talk to me."

2. 这所大学的教学质量很高，不仅如此，它也有很先进的电脑设备。

（這所大學的教學質量很高，不僅如此，它也有很先進的電腦設備。）

"The quality of teaching in this university is very good. In addition to this, the university has advanced computer equipment."

五. 要是... （的话） /要是...的話 *conjunction*: if... This is a conjunction introducing a conditional clause.

1. 要是我很有钱的话，我就去中国旅游。

（要是我很有錢的話，我就去中國旅游。）

"If I had a lot of money, I would travel in China."

2. 你要是喜欢那本书，为什么不买一本呢？

（你要是喜歡那本書，為什麼不買一本呢？）

"If you like that book, why don't you buy it?"

3. 要是在美国，这事一定能办成。

（要是在美國，這事一定能辦成。）

"If this were in America, such a thing could definitely be accomplished."

六. 不管怎么说/不管怎麼説 *adverbial phrase*: in any case, no matter what

1. 不管怎么说，我们都得把凶手找到。

（不管怎麼説，我們都得把兇手找到。）

"No matter what, we have to find the murderer."

2. 不管怎么说他也是你的父亲，你得听他的话。

（不管怎麼説他也是你的父親，你得聽他的話。）

"No matter what, he is your father and you have to listen to him."

3. 你不管怎么说都沒理，所以就少说几句吧！

（你不管怎麼説都沒理，所以就少説幾句吧！）

"In any case, it is your fault, so you'd better keep quiet."

【语法/語法】

尊称
(Honorific Forms)

The most frequently used honorific form in Mandarin Chinese is nín 您, a second person singular pronoun. Its regular form is nǐ 你. Traditionally, the honorific form is used when one addresses someone who is older or a scholar to show respect. For instance, when students address their teachers, or children address their parents or grandparents, they use the honorific form. This is considered proper behavior. Nowadays, however, the functions of the honorific form have been expanded to a certain extent. That is, one can use 您 to address anyone who serves him/her or who does something for him or her, so that the addressee knows whatever s/he does is appreciated. In this case, the addressee does not have to be older than the speaker, nor his/her boss or teacher.

The situation which occurs in the text of this lesson is a good example. Notice that the salesperson addresses his/her customer with the honorific form, but the customer does not respond with the same form. Obviously, this is determined by the relationship between the two persons. It is well known that when a salesperson wants to sell his or her product, s/he is normally polite, enthusiastic, and patient. This applies to the MCI salesperson in the text. S/he wants the customer to join MCI. S/he wants to give the customer an impression of good service and show his/her respect to the customer, but the customer probably does not care about his/her own way of speaking because s/he does not need to (if s/he does not have the habit). Therefore, s/he uses the regular second person pronoun.

【补充词汇/補充詞彙】

服饰、鞋等用品/服飾、鞋等用品(Names of clothes, shoes, and accessories--All the following words are nouns):

长裤（長裤）	chángkù	pants
短裤（裤）	duǎnkù	shorts
牛仔裤（裤）	niúzǎikù	jeans
裙子	qúnzi	skirt
背心	bèixīn	vest
衬衫（襯）	chènshān	shirt/blouse
汗衫	hànshān	undershirt
内衣	nèiyī	underwear
内裤（裤）	nèikù	underpants
睡衣	shuìyī	pajamas
胸罩	xiōngzhào	bra
西装（裝）	xīzhuāng	suit
领带（領）	lǐngdài	tie
燕尾服	yànwěifú	tail-coat
晚礼服（禮）	wǎnlǐfú	evening gown
大衣	dàyī	overcoat
雨衣	yǔyī	raincoat
风衣（風）	fēngyī	windbreaker
毛衣	máoyī	sweater
套头毛衣（頭）	tàotóumáoyī	pullover
高领毛衣（領）	gāolǐngmáoyī	turtleneck pullover
游泳裤（裤）	yóuyǒngkù	swimming trunks
游泳衣	yóuyǒngyī	swimming suit
便鞋	biànxié	loafers
高跟鞋	gāogēnxié	high-heeled shoes

凉鞋（涼）	liángxié	sandals
皮鞋	píxié	leather shoes
拖鞋	tuōxié	slippers
鞋带	xiédài	shoelaces
靴子	xuēzi	boots
半筒袜	bàntǒngwà	knee-high socks
袜子	wàzi	socks
扣子	kòuzi	button
腰带	yāodài	belt
帽子	màozi	hat
手套	shǒutào	gloves
围巾（圍）	wéijīn	scarf
手帕	shǒupà	handkerchief
耳环（鐶）	ěrhuán	earrings
项链（項鍊）	xiàngliàn	necklace
手镯（鐲）	shǒuzhuó	bracelet
戒指	jièzhǐ	finger rings

【练习】

一. 完成句子

　　1. 要是我是推销员的话，＿＿＿＿＿＿＿＿＿＿＿＿＿＿＿＿＿＿＿。

　　2. ＿＿＿＿＿＿＿＿＿＿＿＿＿＿　不仅如此，他跟谁都是油腔滑调的。

　　3. 为了学生方便，＿＿＿＿＿＿＿＿＿＿＿＿＿＿＿＿＿＿＿。

　　4. 他每天都穿西服、打领带，显得 ＿＿＿＿＿＿＿＿＿＿＿＿＿。

　　5. 我常常去那家餐馆吃饭。他们的饭菜和点心都是一流的，不仅如

　　此，＿＿＿＿＿＿＿＿＿＿＿＿＿＿＿＿＿＿＿。

二. 造句：

　　1. 有史以来

　　2. 不管怎么说

　　3. 一会儿...一会儿...

　　4. 任何...都...

　　5. 要是

三. 选词填空：

一会儿…，一会儿　不仅如此　看上去　可是　实际上
但是　特别是

在美国的超级市场和百货商场，服务员对顾客都很客气。买什么东西都
很方便。 _____ 有的时候我还不太习惯。比方说，很多东西的价格
_____ 高， _____ 便宜， _____ ，有的时候买东西还要讨价还
价。在美国生活离不开汽车， _____ 我最不喜欢的是买车， _____
买旧车，有些卖车的人 _____ 热情洋溢， _____ 唯利是图，常常
骗人。

四. 作文：谈谈给你印象最深的广告。你为什么还记得它？

【練習】

一. 完成句子

1. 要是我是推銷員的話，_____。

2. _____ 不僅如此，他跟誰都是油腔滑調的。

3. 為了學生方便，_____。

4. 他每天都穿西服、打領帶，顯得 _____。

5. 我常常去那家餐館吃飯。他們的飯菜和點心都是一流的，不僅如

   此，_____。

二. 造句：

1. 有史以來

2. 不管怎麼說

3. 一會兒…一會兒…

4. 任何…都…

5. 要是

三. 選詞填空：

　　　一會兒…，一會兒　不僅如此　看上去　可是　實際上
　　但是　特別是

在美國的超級市場和百貨商場，服務員對顧客都很客氣。買甚麼東西都
很方便。＿＿＿＿＿＿ 有的時候我還不太習慣。比方說，很多東西的價格
＿＿＿＿＿＿ 高，＿＿＿＿＿＿ 便宜，＿＿＿＿＿＿，有的時候買東西還要討價還
價。在美國生活離不開汽車，＿＿＿＿＿＿ 我最不喜歡的是買車，＿＿＿＿＿＿
買舊車，有些賣車的人 ＿＿＿＿＿＿ 熱情洋溢，＿＿＿＿＿＿ 唯利是圖，常常
騙人。

四. 作文：談談給你印象最深的廣告。你為甚麼還記得它？

【衍生活动】

讨论广告

请在下列广告词中选出两则最有吸引力的，并说明为什么它们能说服人们购买这些产品。

1. 一家烤肉，万家香。（酱油）
2. 要刮别人的胡子吗？先把自己的刮干净！（刮胡刀）
3. 好东西要与好朋友分享。（咖啡）
4. 别让您的孩子输在起跑线上。（儿童英语补习班）
5. 好香好浓的味道！（奶粉）
6. 学琴的孩子不会变坏。（音乐班）
7. 把特别的爱给特别的你。（爱国宣传）
8. 为家里每一张口解渴。（茶）
9. 只要我喜欢有什么不可以。（饮料）
10. 不湿不漏，宝宝开心。（尿布）

【衍生活動】

討論廣告

請在下列廣告詞中選出兩則最有吸引力的，並說明為甚麼它們能說服人們購買這些產品。

1. 一家烤肉，萬家香。（醬油）
2. 要刮別人的鬍子嗎？先把自己的刮乾淨！（刮鬍刀）
3. 好東西要與好朋友分享。（咖啡）
4. 別讓您的孩子輸在起跑線上。（兒童英語補習班）
5. 好香好濃的味道！（奶粉）
6. 學琴的孩子不會變壞。（音樂班）
7. 把特別的愛給特別的你。（愛國宣傳）
8. 為家裡每一張口解渴。（茶）
9. 只要我喜歡有甚麼不可以。（飲料）
10. 不濕不漏，寶寶開心。（尿布）

【第四課】

各行各業

【课文】

各行各业

甲： 我是律师，您是做什么工作的？

乙： 我是教书的。做我们这种工作，整天吃粉笔灰，每个月领固定的薪水，饿不死却也富不了，不像你们律师，能赚很多钱。

甲： 不要这麽讲嘛，当律师钱可能是多点儿，可是这钱来之不易啊！干我们这行的要早起晚睡，辛苦极了。哪有你们教师那么轻松自在。

乙： 事实可不像你想的那样。当老师也没什么自在的，我们除了教书以外，还得搞科研。如果论文发表得不够，就有被解雇的危险。当然我说的是美国的情形，在中国，教师可能没有这个问题。你们当律师的在美国也没有这个问题。

甲： 你既然觉得律师这个职业好，当初你为什么不选择这行呢？

乙： 那是因为我不愿意让人们骂。我常听到有人骂律师是骗子。虽然当老师有很多坏处，但是至少比较受人尊敬，不用被人骂。

甲： 实际上，什么行业都有好人，有坏人。有人说律师的坏话，不等于所有的律师都不好，至少我还没听到人骂我。

乙： 你怎么这么天真？难道别人会当着你的面骂你吗？

甲： 算了，算了，不跟你争了。最后只想提醒你，中国有句俗

话：三百六十行，行行出状元。只要好好干，总有出头的
一天。

乙： 这话倒是没错，不过人总是干一行怨一行。

讨论题：

你认为什么职业最好？为什么？

【課文】

各行各業

甲： 我是律師，您是做甚麼工作的？

乙： 我是教書的。做我們這種工作，整天吃粉筆灰，每個月領固定的薪水，餓不死卻也富不了，不像你們律師，能賺很多錢。

甲： 不要這麼講嘛，當律師錢可能是多點兒，可是這錢來之不易啊！幹我們這行的要早起晚睡，辛苦極了。哪有你們教師那麼輕鬆自在。

乙： 事實可不像你想的那樣。當老師也沒甚麼自在的，我們除了教書以外，還得搞科研。如果論文發表得不夠，就有被解雇的危險。當然我說的是美國的情形，在中國，教師可能沒有這個問題。你們當律師的在美國也沒有這個問題。

甲： 你既然覺得律師這個職業好，當初你為甚麼不選擇這行呢？

乙： 那是因為我不願意讓人們罵。我常聽到有人罵律師是騙子。雖然當老師有很多壞處，但是至少比較受人尊敬，不用被人罵。

甲： 實際上，甚麼行業都有好人，有壞人。有人說律師的壞話，不等於所有的律師都不好，至少我還沒聽到人罵我。

乙： 你怎麼這麼天真？難道別人會當着你的面罵你嗎？

甲： 算了，算了，不跟你爭了。最後只想提醒你，中國有句俗

話：三百六十行，行行出狀元。只要好好幹，總有出頭的
一天。

乙： 這話倒是沒錯，不過人總是幹一行怨一行。

討論題：

你認為甚麼職業最好？為甚麼？

【生词/生詞】

1. 各行各业（業）	gèhánggèyè	n.p.	every field of work
2. 律师（師）	lǜshī	n.	lawyer
3. 整天	zhěngtiān	adv.	all day long
4. 粉笔（筆）	fěnbǐ	n.	chalk
5. 灰	huī	n.	dust, ash
6. 赚（賺）	zhuàn	v.	to earn, to make (money)
7. 来之不易（來）	láizhībúyì	v.p.	not easy to obtain
8. 早起晚睡	zǎoqǐwǎnshuì	v.p.	to get up early & go to bed late
9. 辛苦	xīnkǔ	adj.	(to be) laborious
10. 轻松（輕鬆）	qīngsōng	adj.	(to be) relaxed
11. 自在	zìzài	adj.	(to be) unconstrained
12. 事实（實）	shìshí	n.	fact
13. 搞	gǎo	v.	to do (e.g. research)
14. 科研	kēyán	n.	scientific research
15. 论文（論）	lùnwén	n.	research paper, dissertation
16. 发表（發）	fābiǎo	v.	to publish (articles)
17. 解雇	jiěgù	v.	to fire, to dismiss
18. 危险（險）	wēixiǎn	n./adj.	danger; (to be) dangerous
19. 情形	qíngxíng	n.	situation
20. 职业（職業）	zhíyè	n.	occupation
21. 愿意（願）	yuànyì	aux.	to be willing to
22. 骗子（騙）	piànzi	n.	swindler, trickster
23. 受	shòu	v.	passive marker; to receive
24. 尊敬	zūnjìng	v.\n.	to respect; respect
25. 实际上（實際）	shíjìshàng	adv.p.	in fact
26. 等于（於）	děngyú	v.	to be equal to
27. 天真	tiānzhēn	adj.	(to be) naive, innocent
28. 算了	suànle	v.p.	Forget it!

29. 争〔爭〕	zhēng	v.	to fight, to argue
30. 提醒	tíxǐng	v.	to remind
31. 俗话〔話〕	súhuà	n.	common saying
32. 怨	yuàn	v.	to blame

【句型】

一. 是......的 *verb phrase*: This construction is often used to describe what people do.

　　1. 我父亲是做生意的。

　　　（我父親是做生意的。）

　　　"My father does business (or is a businessman)."

　　2. 他的孩子都是研究中国文学的。

　　　（他的孩子都是研究中國文學的。）

　　　"All of his children are doing research on Chinese literature."

二. 为什么不/為甚麼不+ VP? *rhetorical question*: Why not ...? This construction is used to offer strong suggestions.

　　1. 为什么不去？那个地方很有意思。

　　　（為甚麼不去？那個地方很有意思。）

　　　"Why don't you go? That is a very interesting place."

　　2. 他病得那么厉害，为什么不把他送到医院去呢？

　　　（他病得那麼厲害，為甚麼不把他送到醫院去呢？）

　　　"He is very sick; why don't you send him to the hospital?"

　　3. 既然你那么爱他，为什么不跟他结婚呢？

　　　（既然你那麼愛他，爲甚麼不跟他結婚呢？）

　　　"If you love him so much, why don't you marry him?"

三. 当初/當初 *adverb*: originally, in the first place. This phrase is often used as part of the time-contrast structure.

　　1. 当初他很穷，可是现在却成了百万富翁。

（當初他很窮，可是現在卻成了百萬富翁。）

"He was very poor at the beginning, but now he is a millionaire."

2. 既然你这么不喜欢教书，当初为什么选择当老师呢？

（既然你這麼不喜歡教書，當初為甚麼選擇當老師呢？）

"You don't like teaching at all; so why did you choose to be a teacher in the first place."

四. 至少 *adverb*: at least

1. 这个工作不太好，可至少我不必整天在家呆着。

（這個工作不太好，可至少我不必整天在家呆著。）

"Although this job is not very good, at least I don't have to stay home all day."

2. 这本书至少要花二十块才能买到。

（這本書至少要花二十塊才能買到。）

"This book costs at least twenty dollars."

五. 不等于（不等於）　*verb phrase*: not equal to; do not mean that

1. 五加六不等于十。

（五加六不等於十。）

"Five plus six is not equal to ten."

2. 他沒来不等于他不喜欢你。

（他沒來不等於他不喜歡你。）

"His not coming does not mean he does not like you."

六. 难道/難道 *verb phrase*: Are you telling me that ...? It is a rhetorical question expressing speakers' disbelief in something.

1. 难道我们得养你一辈子吗？

（難道我們得養你一輩子嗎？）

"Are you telling me that I have to feed you for the rest of your life?"

2. 难道你真是个骗子不成？

（難道你真是個騙子不成？）

"Is it really true that you are a swindler?"

【语法/語法】

被动式/被動式
(Passive Constructions)

The passive construction in Chinese has the form: NP1 + 被 + (NP2) + Verb. In most cases, NP1 is the patient or receiver of the action of the verb, and NP2, which is optional, is the agent of the verb's action. The morpheme 被 is a function word. In classical Chinese, the whole construction was used to express the meaning of adversity only. That is, something bad happens to the patient, as in 1-2:

1. 他被人打了。 （他被人打了。）

   "He was beaten by someone."

2. 他被逼得卖儿卖女。 （他被逼得賣兒賣女。）

   "He was forced to sell his children."

In modern Chinese, however, the use of the passive construction is not limited to that interpretation anymore. They have been increasingly used to express neutral and positive meaning as well. For instance:

3. 他被选为市长了。 （他被選為市長了。）

   "He was elected mayor."

4. 她被她的同学当成模范。 （她被她的同學當成模範。）

   "She is treated as a model by her classmates."

Studies show that the increasing use of the 被 construction expressing positive meaning has been affected by passive constructions in European languages like English. Furthermore, researchers point out that this does not mean that Chinese passives are functionally the same as English passives. Students should pay special attention to the types of Chinese passives that can or cannot be interpreted as English passives and vice versa.

The function word 被 sometimes can be replaced by other words, such as 给 （給）, 让 （讓）, etc. For instance:

5. 我们被/让他的话感动了。 （我們被/讓他的話感動了。）

   "We were touched by his words."

6. 他给/让/被人骗了。 （他給/讓/被人騙了。）

   "He was cheated by someone."

However, students should be aware that 给 （給） and 让 （讓） have many other functions and cannot always be used in passive constructions.

【补充词汇/補充詞彙】

表示职业的名词/表示職業的名詞(All of the following words are nouns of professions):

编辑 （編輯）	biānjí	editor
厨师 （廚師）	chúshī	chef
法官	fǎguān	judge
歌星	gēxīng	star-singer
工程师 （師）	gōngchéngshī	engineer
护士 （護）	hùshì	nurse
记者 （記）	jìzhě	reporter
建筑师 （築師） *	jiànzhùshī	architect
教练 （練）	jiàoliàn	coach
警察	jǐngchá	police
科学家 （學） *	kēxuéjiā	scientist
会计 （會計）	kuàijì	accountant
秘书 （書）	mìshū	secretary
尼姑	nígū	nun
清洁工 （潔）	qīngjiégōng	janitor
摄影师 （攝師） *	shèyǐngshī	photographer
推销员 （銷員）	tuīxiāoyuán	salesperson
图书管员 （圖書、員）	túshūguǎnyuán	librarian
校长 （長）	xiàozhǎng	president (school)
研究员 （員）	yánjiūyuán	researcher
音乐家 （樂） *	yīnyuèjiā	musician
艺术家 （藝術） *	yìshùjiā	artist
演员 （員）	yǎnyuán	performer
运动员 （運動員）	yùndòngyuán	athlete
总统 （總統）	zǒngtǒng	president

*The words 家 and 师 （師） in these words contain the connotation of being authorative in the field.

【练习】

一. 用所给的词语回答问题：

　　1. 你知道不知道张教授做什么研究？（是...的）

　　2. 听说在中国做买卖的赚的钱最多，是吗？（早起晚睡）

　　3. 他看上去很诚实，为什么他的同学都不太喜欢他呢？（说...坏话）

　　4. 你每天练习几个小时的中文？（至少）

　　5. 在中国当老师有什么好处？（轻松自在、受）

二. 造句：

　　1. 当初

　　2. 为什么不

　　3. 不等于

　　4. 难道

5. 实际上

三. 把下面的句子改成"被"、"让"、或"给"字句，并说明两种句式在意义上的不同。

1. 那个油腔滑调的推销员骗了很多人。

2. 我以为我猜出了李教授的背景，其实我猜错了。

3. 虽然王律师为了工作每天早起晚睡，老板还是把他解雇了。

4. 自作聪明的图书馆员把书弄乱了。

5. 他们撤消了那个贪得无厌的校长的职务。

四. 选词填空：

不得已　职业　有史以来　可是　早起晚睡

据说，现在中国人最想干的 _____ 是作买卖，当老板。很多教授也想"下海"。"下海"就是作买卖的意思。 _____ 中国的知识分子都是受尊敬的，为什么现在他们不想再教书了呢？原因是他们整天都辛苦地工作， _____， _____ 他们的工资很低。他们一边教书一边作买卖也是 _____ 的。

五. 作文：谈谈作买卖（或者其它职业）的甘苦 (150字左右)

The following structures should be useful for you to construct cohesive paragraphs:

1. Listing Structure:

_____ 作 _____ 工作，整天不是 _____

就是 _____ ，要不然 _____

_____。

2. Comparison Structure:

当 _____ 不像 _____

那么 _____ 比如，_____

当 _____ 的 _____。

可是，当 _____ 的 _____。

【練習】

一. 用所給的詞語回答問題：

　　1. 你知道不知道張教授做甚麼研究？（是...的）

　　2. 聽說在中國做買賣的賺的錢最多，是嗎？（早起晚睡）

　　3. 他看上去很誠實，為甚麼他的同學都不太喜歡他呢？（說...壞話）

　　4. 你每天練習幾個小時的中文？（至少）

　　5. 在中國當老師有甚麼好處？（輕鬆自在、受）

二. 造句：

　　1. 當初

　　2. 為甚麼不

　　3. 不等於

　　4. 難道

5. 實際上

三. 把下面的句子改成 "被"、"讓"、或 "給" 字句, 並說明兩種句式在意義上的不同:

1. 那個油腔滑調的推銷員騙了很多人。

2. 我以為我猜出了李教授的背景, 其實我猜錯了。

3. 雖然王律師為了工作每天早起晚睡, 老板還是把他解雇了。

4. 自作聰明的圖書館員把書弄亂了。

5. 他們撤消了那個貪得無厭的校長的職務。

四. 選詞填空:

　　不得已　職業　有史以來　可是　早起晚睡

據說, 現在中國人最想幹的 ＿＿＿＿＿ 是作買賣, 當老板。很多教授也想 "下海"。"下海" 就是作買賣的意思。＿＿＿＿＿ 中國的知識分子都是受尊敬的, 為甚麼現在他們不想再教書了呢? 原因是他們整天都辛苦地工作, ＿＿＿＿＿, ＿＿＿＿＿ 他們的工資很低。他們一邊教書一邊作買賣也是 ＿＿＿＿＿ 的。

五. 作文：談談作買賣〔或者其它職業〕的甘苦 (150字左右)

The following structures should be useful for you to construct cohesive paragraphs:

1. Listing Structure:

_____ 作 _____ 工作，整天不是 _____
就是 _____，要不然_____
_____。

2. Comparison Structure:

當 _____ 不像 _____ 那麼
_____ 比如，_____
當 _____ 的 _____。可是，
當 _____ 的 _____。

【衍生活动】

解决难题

校长的难题：

　　你是一个大学的校长，现在学校经费(budget)不够。你需要裁掉(eliminate)五个系。你会裁掉哪些系？为什么？请在课前查出常见科系名称，并在课堂上说明你裁掉这些科系的标准与理由。

常见大学科系名称：

教育	人类学	物理	宗教	国际关系
历史	心理学	化学	艺术	东亚研究
会计	航海	数学	法律	图书馆学
生物	语言学	政治	经济	中国文学
建筑	环境工程	电脑	航空	企业管理

【衍生活動】

解決難題

校長的難題：

　　你是一個大學的校長，現在學校經費(budget)不夠。你需要裁掉(eliminate)五個系。你會裁掉哪些系？為甚麼？請在課前查出常見科系名稱，並在課堂上說明你裁掉這些科系的標準與理由。

常見大學科系名稱：

教育	人類學	物理	宗教	國際關係
歷史	心理學	化學	藝術	東亞研究
會計	航海	數學	法律	圖書館學
生物	語言學	政治	經濟	中國文學
建築	環境工程	電腦	航空	企業管理

中國文學：無用

語言學：無聊

【第五課】

難題二、三則

【课文】

难题二、三则

难题之一：

一个老外在餐厅点了一盘麻婆豆腐，菜来了发现豆腐的味道有点怪，好像坏了，怎么跟服务员理论？

人物： 甲=倒霉的老外， 乙=女服务员， 丙=餐厅老板

甲： 小姐，这盘豆腐有点儿怪味儿，好像是豆腐坏了。

乙： 不会吧？我们这里从来不用过期的豆腐，怎么会坏呢？

甲： 你不信，可以亲自尝尝，

乙： 你要是不喜欢吃豆腐，就点点儿别的，我没必要尝你的菜。

甲： 我不是那个意思，我很喜欢豆腐，只是这盘吃着不对劲，
你能不能给换一盘？

乙： 当然可以，可是你得再付钱。

甲： 为什么？难道坏豆腐也得付钱吗？

乙： 这盘菜你已经吃了不少，当然要付钱。

甲： 你这个人真不讲理，我要跟你们老板说说。

乙： 你爱跟谁说就跟谁说吧！反正我不能白给你一个菜。

（找到了老板。）

甲： 这个服务员真不像话。

丙： 怎么回事？

甲： 我告诉他这盘豆腐有点怪味儿，想让他给换一换，他不但不给换，反而出口伤人。

丙： 先生，您别生气，我马上让人给您换一盘，您不必再付钱。

甲： 好吧，谢谢你。

丙： 有什么意见，请随时告诉我。菜来了，请您慢慢享用。

难题之二：

你对餐厅的服务或者饭菜不满意，跟餐厅的工作人员说了几次都没有用，然后怎么办？

难题之三：

你的老板给你的工作越来越多，可是薪水从来没有调整过，你想请老板给你加薪水，该怎么开口？

难题之四：

你是一个家教，最近你发现你的学生的功课一落千丈，因为他恨高考，恨教育制度，他觉得父母都不了解他，甚至觉得生命没有价值，你怎么跟他谈？

难题之五：

你的老师非常认真，但是有一点固执，你对他的教法不太适应，你想告诉他，但是又不想伤他的心，你该怎么跟他说？

难题之六：

你认为你的男（女）朋友跟自己性格不合，想提出跟他分手的要求，但是又不想伤害对方，该怎么开口？

【課文】

難題二、三則

難題之一：

一個老外在餐廳點了一盤麻婆豆腐，菜來了發現豆腐的味道有點怪，好像壞了，怎麼跟服務員理論？

人物： 甲＝倒霉的老外， 乙＝女服務員， 丙＝餐廳老板

甲： 小姐，這盤豆腐有點兒怪味兒，好像是豆腐壞了。

乙： 不會吧？我們這裏從來不用過期的豆腐，怎麼會壞呢？

甲： 你不信，可以親自嘗嘗。

乙： 你要是不喜歡吃豆腐，就點點兒別的，我沒必要嘗你的菜。

甲： 我不是那個意思，我很喜歡豆腐，只是這盤吃着不對勁，你能不能給換一盤？

乙： 當然可以，可是你得再付錢。

甲： 為甚麼？難道壞豆腐也得付錢嗎？

乙： 這盤菜你已經吃了不少，當然要付錢。

甲： 你這個人真不講理，我要跟你們老板說說。

乙： 你愛跟誰說就跟誰說吧！反正我不能白給你一個菜。

（找到了老板。）

甲： 這個服務員真不像話。

丙： 怎麼回事？

甲： 我告訴他這盤豆腐有點怪味兒，想讓他給換一換，他不但不給換，反而出口傷人。

丙： 先生，您別生氣，我馬上讓人給您換一盤，您不必再付錢。

甲： 好吧，謝謝你。

丙： 有甚麼意見，請隨時告訴我。菜來了，請您慢慢享用。

難題之二：
你對餐廳的服務或者飯菜不滿意，跟餐廳的工作人員說了幾次都沒有用，然後怎麼辦？

難題之三：
你的老板給你的工作越來越多，可是薪水從來沒有調整過，你想請老板給你加薪水，該怎麼開口？

難題之四：
你是一個家教，最近你發現你的學生的功課一落千丈，因為他恨高考，恨教育制度，他覺得父母都不了解他，甚至覺得生命沒有價值，你怎麼跟他談？

難題之五：
你的老師非常認真，但是有一點固執，你對他的教法不太適應，你想告訴他，但是又不想傷他的心，你該怎麼跟他說？

難題之六：
你認為你的男（女）朋友跟自己性格不合，想提出跟他分手的要求，但是又不想傷害對方，該怎麼開口？

【生词/生詞】

1. 老外	lǎowài	n.	foreigner (colloq.)
2. 餐厅（餐廳）	cāntīng	n.	dining hall
3. 麻婆豆腐	mápódòufǔ	n.p.	tofu cooked with peppercorns
4. 味道	wèidào	n.	taste
5. 倒霉	dǎoméi	adj.	(to be) unlucky
6. 怪味(儿)	guàiwèi(er)	n.	strange taste or smell
7. 理论（論）	lǐlùn	v./n.	to reason; theory
8. 过期（過）	guòqī	v.	to pass the expiration date, to be overdue
9. 亲自	qīnzì	adv.	by oneself
10. 尝（嘗）	cháng	v.	to taste
11. 点（點）	diǎn	v.	to order (dishes)
12. 必要	bìyào	adj.	(to be) necessary
13. 对劲（對勁）	duìjìn	adj.	(to feel) right (colloq.)
14. 付钱（錢）	fùqián	v.p.	to pay
15. 讲理（講）	jiǎnglǐ	v.	to reason
16. 反正	fǎnzhèng	adv.	in any case, anyway
17. 白	bái	adv.	for nothing, in vain
18. 出口伤人（傷）	chūkǒushāngrén	v.p.	to use hurtful language
19. 随时（隨時）	suíshí	adv.	at any time
20. 享用	xiǎngyòng	v.	to enjoy eating
21. 薪水	xīnshuǐ	n.	wage
22. 调整（調）	tiáozhěng	v.	to adjust
23. 家教	jiājiào	n.	private tutor
24. 一落千丈	yīluòqiānzhàng	v.p.	to suffer a disastrous decline
25. 高考	gāokǎo	n.	college entrance exam
26. 固执（執）	gùzhí	adj.	(to be) stubborn
27. 伤害（傷）	shānghài	v.	to hurt

【句型】

一. **不对劲/不對勁** *verb phrase*: something must be wrong; not to be right

  1. 小李今天不对劲，好像发生了什么事。

   （小李今天不對勁，好像發生了甚麼事。）

   "Little Li does not look right today. It seems something has happened."

  2. 这支曲子听起来不对劲，是不是什么地方改了。

   （這支曲子聽起來不對勁，是不是甚麼地方改了。）

   "Something must be wrong with this music. Has any part of it changed?"

  3. 我看他们俩最近不太对劲，是不是已经分手了。

   （我看他們倆最近不太對勁，是不是已經分手了。）

   "I don't think those two look right lately. Have they broken?"

二. **爱/愛** + VP **就** + VP; *adverb* +*VP*: to do whatever one wants

  1. 你爱怎么说就怎么说，反正我不理你。

   （你愛怎麼說就怎麼說，反正我不理你。）

   "You can say whatever you want; however, I don't want to talk to you."

  2. 他爱怎么作，就怎么作吧！孩子大了，已经不好管了。

   （他愛怎麼作，就怎麼作吧！孩子大了，已經不好管了。）

   "You can do whatever you want. You are grown-up now and not easy to

   discipline anymore."

  3. 你爱看什么书都行，就是不要看黄书。

   （你愛看什麼書都行，就是不要看黃書。）

   "You can read whatever books you want, except for pornography books."

三. **反正** *adverb*: in any case

  1. 他从来不说实话，不管你信不信，反正我不信他的话。

   （他從來不說實話，不管你信不信，反正我不信他的話。）

   "He never tells the truth. Regardless of whether you trust him or not,

   I don't trust him."

2. 我不喜欢那个地方，无论你怎么说，我反正不去。

（我不喜歡那個地方，無論你怎麼說，我反正不去。）

"I don't like that place. No matter what you say, I am not going."

3. 反正我是你的儿子，你不能把我赶出去。

（反正我是你的兒子，你不能把我趕出去。）

"In any case, I am your son, and you cannot kick me out."

四. 白 *adverb*: free of charge, for nothing, in vain

1. 餐厅的饭你不能白吃，你得付钱。

（餐廳的飯你不能白吃，你得付錢。）

"You have to pay for the meals, because they are not free."

2. 昨天我到书店的时候，书店已经关门了，所以我白去了一趟。

（昨天我到書店的時候，書店已經關門了，所以我白去了一趟。）

"When I went to the bookstore yesterday, it was already closed, so I went there in vain."

3. 他已经跟别人结婚了，我白白等了他五年。

（他已經跟別人結婚了，我白白等了他五年。）

"He already married someone else; I waited five years for him in vain."

五. （对）...不适应/（對）...不適應 *verb phrase*: not fit; not adapt to...

1. 我对这里的天气不太适应。

（我對這裏的天氣不太適應。）

"I have not adapted to the weather here."

2. 我对老师的教学方法不太适应。

（我對老師的教學方法不太適應。）

"I have not adapted myself to the teacher's teaching style."

3. 张先生不适应当老师。

（張先生不適應當老師。）

"This teaching job does not suit Mr. Zhang."

【语法/語法】

称呼/稱呼
(How to Address Someone)

In the previous lesson, we discussed the use of honorific forms. Now let us see how to address someone in different social settings. First of all, it should be pointed out that ways of addressing different people in Mandarin Chinese have changed a number of times since the beginning of the twentieth century. (This is the case in mainland China.)

During the 1920's-1930's, the most commonly used terms to address one another in the middle and high classes were 先生 "Mister", 太太 "Mistress", or 小姐 "Miss" with one's last name preceding these terms (for instance: 王先生，李太太). This was also true when husbands and wives referred to their spouse when talking to someone. The only difference between addressing someone and referring to one's spouse was that the latter used the first person pronoun before those terms, such as 我先生/太太, whereas the former used one's last name. In the lower class or rural areas, husbands often referred to their wives as 老婆 or 家里（裡）人; wives often referred to their husbands as 当（當）家的.

From 1950's to early 1980's, 先生 and 太太 were no longer common; instead 同志 "comrade" became the most popular term used to address one another (it could be used to address anyone: male, female, married, unmarried). During the late 1970's and early 1980's, 师（師）傅 "master" was often heard in public areas, such as in shops, at market, on trains, etc. It was primarily used to address someone whom the addresser did not know, but from whom the addresser received help or services. Like 同志, 师（師）傅 did not have a gender distinction either. During this period of time, both husband and wife referred to their spouse as 爱（愛）人 "the loved one". It should be noted that these new terms did not penetrate rural areas so much as cities; most peasants still used the old terms mentioned above.

Interestingly, starting in the 1980's, 先生 and 太太 became popular again in public settings. When travelling to China now, you are very likely to hear people address you using your surname+先生/太太, not 同志.

Students should know that there are two other ways which are commonly used to address someone. They are 老+one's surname and 小+one's surname. These ways of addressing someone started at approximately the beginning of this century and are still frequently used among common people. The choice of the two is conditioned by the addressee's age: if the addressee is about forty years old or younger, s/he is likely to be addressed by his/her colleagues as 小+his/her surname; otherwise s/he will be addressed as 老+his/her surname. With this brief sketch of the development of terms used to address someone, students get a glimpse of one aspect of Chinese sociolinguistics, or rather, one aspect of Chinese society.

【补充辞汇/補充辭彙】

建议（議）	jiànyì	v./n.	to suggest; suggestion
劝（勸）	quàn	v.	to advise
诺言（諾）	nuòyán	n.	promise
违背（違）	wéibèi	v.	to break (a promise)
提出	tíchū	v.	to put forward
抱歉	bàoqiàn	v.	to apologize
原谅（諒）	yuánliàng	v.	to forgive
对…不满（對）	duì…bùmǎn	v.p.	to feel unsatisfied with
抱怨	duì…bàoyuàn	v.	to complain about
对…提出控告	duì…tíchūkònggào	v.p.	to bring a complaint against
对…提出抗议（議）	duì…tíchūkàngyì	v.p.	to protest against
发牢骚（發，騷）	fāláosāo	v.p.	to grumble
发怒（發）	fānù	v.	to become angry
愤怒（憤）	fènnù	adj.	(to be) very angry
讨厌（討厭）	tǎoyàn	v.	to be disgusting
公平	gōngpíng	adj.	(to be) fair
不讲理（講）	bùjiǎnglǐ	v.p	to be unreasonable
不像话（話）	búxiànghuà	v.p.	That's outrageous!
关你什么事（關）	guānnǐshénmeshì	v.p.	None of your business!
发脾气（發，氣）	fāpíqì	v.p.	to lose temper
他妈的	tāmāde	adj.p.	Damn it!
狗屁	gǒupì	n.	bullshit
滚开（開）	gǔnkāi	v.	Get lost!
讨厌鬼（討厭）	tǎoyànguǐ	n.	jerk
小气鬼（氣）	xiǎoqìguǐ	n.	cheapskate
伪君子（僞）	wěijūnzǐ	n.	hypocrite
老油条（條）	lǎoyóutiáo	n.	old fox
畜生	chùshēng	n.	beast (swear word)

【练习】

一. 完成句子：

1. _____ 是因为我不想伤他的心。

2. 要是对餐厅的饭菜不满意，你随时 _____。

3. 他最近的学习成绩一落千丈，好像 _____。

4. 他的老板真不像话，_____。

5. 老板给我的工作越来越多，他不但不给我加工资，反而 _____

_____。

二. 造句：
1. 反正

2. 跟...不合

3. 爱...就 ...

4. 要是

5. 对...不适应

三. 用所给词回答问题：

1. 如果你点的菜越吃越不对劲，你会怎么办？（白＋VERB, 假如，换，付钱）

3. 很多公司现在喜欢用电话推销他们的产品，你对此有什么看法？（反正，对...不适应，不仅如此，要是）

四. 作文：给老师的几点建议 (You would like to suggest some changes about the teaching methods or teaching materials. In order to do this, you need to justify first why the suggested changes are necessary. You will find the following words or phrases useful: 调整，对...不适应，不必，要是，提出，建议，要求，虽然)

【練習】

一. 完成句子：

1. _____ 是因為我不想傷他的心。

2. 要是對餐廳的飯菜不滿意，你隨時 _____。

3. 他最近的學習成績一落千丈，好像 _____。

4. 他的老板真不像話，_____。

5. 老板給我的工作越來越多，他不但不給我加工資，反而 _____

_____。

二. 造句：
1. 反正

2. 跟...不合

3. 愛...就 ...

4. 要是

5. 對...不適應

三. 用所給詞回答問題：

1. 如果你點的菜越吃越不對勁，你會怎麼辦？ （白＋VERB, 假如，換，付錢）

3. 很多公司現在喜歡用電話推銷他們的產品，你對此有甚麼看法？ （反正，對...不適應，不僅如此，要是）

四. 作文：給老師的幾點建議 (You would like to suggest some changes about the teaching methods or teaching materials. In order to do, this you need to justify first why the suggested changes are necessary. You will find the following words or phrases useful: 調整，對...不適應，不必，要是，提出，建議，要求，雖然)

【第六課】

午餐

【课文】

午餐

王先生： 难得老板给大家加薪，一块儿吃顿午饭庆祝庆祝吧！我看您为了把学生教好，每天只吃面包、水果也不是个办法，今天中午给自己放个假吧！

李小姐： 说的也是，最近老觉得头昏，大概是营养不良，有机会换换口味也不错。但是我这个人吃东西挑得很，又不太爱吃肉，我们一块儿吃饭恐怕要委屈您了。

王先生： 您用"委屈"这两个字就太见外了。像我们这种成天坐办公室又不爱运动的人，肉吃多了反而没有好处，再说我平时也吃得很清淡，不过，同事这么多年我还不知道您是吃素的呢！

李小姐： 吃蔬菜确实比吃肉健康。严格地说，我并不是个真正的素食主义者。我吃海鲜，特别是鱼肉，一个星期至少吃两次，补充身体所需要的蛋白质。我最喜欢吃生鱼片，至于虾、螃蟹等等我也一概不忌。

王先生： 好了。言归正传，中午吃什么呢？上素菜馆去，还是吃四川菜？广东菜？江浙菜？你选吧！

李小姐： 既然你让我选，我就直言不讳了，四川菜太辣，广东菜太甜，对面新开的江浙菜馆不错，他们的红烧鱼做得好极了。连一点腥味儿都没有，砂锅豆腐也很地道，既是菜又是汤，如果是两个人吃就再加一个清炒豆芽。那家餐馆最大的优点是不用味精，菜也做得精致，怎么样？上那儿去吧？

王先生： 饭后他们也免费提供甜点、水果吗？听说他们做的豆沙包，芝麻球也是一流的。

李小姐： 他们做的点心的确是一流的，让人百吃不厌，不过不是免费的，你想那么好吃的东西老板会让顾客白吃吗？提到价钱，他们的菜可不便宜。我们各付各的，谁也别请客。

王先生： 老同事你还这么客气，今天我作东，下次轮到你，再推辞你就是不给我面子了。

李小姐： 那我就只好从命了。

讨论题：

1. 谈谈你对李小姐的饮食观的看法。
2. 谈谈你的饮食哲学，你认为吃什么最健康？
3. 就你看来，吃素跟吃肉哪种饮食方式比较健康，为什么？
4. 如果你是素食主义者，请你说明你吃素的理由。
5. 请仔细描述一道菜的作法。
6. 中国人和美国人的饮食方式有什么不同？

【課文】

午餐

王先生： 難得老板給大家加薪，一塊兒吃頓午飯慶祝慶祝吧！我看您為了把學生教好，每天只吃麵包、水果也不是個辦法，今天中午給自己放個假吧！

李小姐： 說的也是，最近老覺得頭昏，大概是營養不良，有機會換換口味也不錯。但是我這個人吃東西挑得很，又不太愛吃肉，我們一塊兒吃飯恐怕要委屈您了。

王先生： 您用"委屈"這兩個字就太見外了。像我們這種成天坐辦公室又不愛運動的人，肉吃多了反而沒有好處，再說我平時也吃得很清淡，不過，同事這麼多年我還不知道您是吃素的呢！

李小姐： 吃蔬菜確實比吃肉健康。嚴格地說，我並不是個真正的素食主義者。我吃海鮮，特別是魚肉，一個星期至少吃兩次，補充身體所需要的蛋白質。我最喜歡吃生魚片，至於蝦、螃蟹等等我也一概不忌。

王先生： 好了。言歸正傳，中午吃甚麼呢？上素菜館去，還是吃四川菜？廣東菜？江浙菜？你選吧！

李小姐： 既然你讓我選，我就直言不諱了，四川菜太辣，廣東菜太甜，對面新開的江浙菜館不錯，他們的紅燒魚做得好極了。連一點腥味兒都沒有，砂鍋豆腐也很地道，既是

菜又是湯，如果是兩個人吃就再加一個清炒豆芽。那家
餐館最大的優點是不用味精，菜也做得精緻，怎麼樣？
上那兒去吧？

王先生：　飯後他們也免費提供甜點、水果嗎？聽說他們做的豆沙
包，芝麻球也是一流的。

李小姐：　他們做的點心的確是一流的，讓人百吃不厭，不過不是
免費的，你想那麼好吃的東西老板會讓顧客白吃嗎？提
到價錢，他們的菜可不便宜。我們各付各的，誰也別請
客。

王先生：　老同事你還這麼客氣，今天我作東，下次輪到你，再推
辭你就是不給我面子了。

李小姐：　那我就只好從命了。

討論題：
1. 談談你對李小姐的飲食觀的看法。
2. 談談你的飲食哲學，你認為吃甚麼最健康？
3. 就你看來，吃素跟吃肉哪種飲食方式比較健康，為甚麼？
4. 如果你是素食主義者，請你說明你吃素的理由。
5. 請仔細描述一道菜的作法。
6. 中國人和美國人的飲食方式有甚麼不同？

【生词/生詞】

1. 加薪	jiāxīn	v.p.	to raise (someone's) salary
2. 庆祝 (慶)	qìngzhù	v.	to celebrate
3. 计划 (計劃)	jìhuà	v./n.	to plan; plan
4. 老	lǎo	adv.	often
5. 头昏 (頭)	tóuhūn	v.	to be dizzy
6. 大概	dàgài	adv.	probably
7. 营养不良 (營養)	yíngyǎngbùliáng	adj.p.	(to be) malnourished
8. 恐怕	kǒngpà	v.	to be afraid of
9. 委屈	wěiqū	v.	to feel wronged
10. 见外 (見)	jiànwài	v.	to regard oneself as an outsider
11. 平时 (時)	píngshí	adv.	ordinarily
12. 清淡	qīngdàn	adj.	(to be) light and delicate
13. 素	sù	adj.	vegetable
14. 确实 (確實)	quèshí	adv.	indeed
15. 海鲜 (鮮)	hǎixiān	n.	seafood
16. 特别	tèbié	adv./adj.	specially; special
17. 补充 (補)	bǔchōng	v./n.	to supplement; supplement
18. 蛋白质 (質)	dànbáizhì	n.	protein
19. 生鱼片 (魚)	shēngyúpiàn	n.p.	raw sliced fish
20. 螃蟹	pángxiè	n.	crab
21. 一概	yígài	adv.	without exception
22. 忌	jì	v.	to restrain from
23. 言归正传 (歸傳)	yánguīzhèngzhuàn	adv.p.	to return to the subject
24. 直言不讳 (不諱)	zhíyánbúhuì	v.p.	to speak bluntly
25. 红烧鱼 (紅燒魚)	hóngshāoyú	n.p.	braised fish with soy sauce
26. 腥味	xīngwèi	n.	smelling of fish

27. 沙锅（鍋）	shāguō	n.	earthenware pot
28. 地道	dìdào	adj.	(to be) authentic
29. 豆芽（芽）	dòuyá	n.	bean sprout
30. 味精	wèijīng	n.	MSG
31. 精致	jīngzhì	adj.	(to be) elegant
32. 提供	tígōng	v.	to provide
33. 甜点（點）	tiándiǎn	n.	sweets
34. 豆沙	dòushā	n.	bean paste
35. 芝麻	zhīmá	n.	sesame
36. 一流	yīliú	adj.	(to be) first class
37. 百吃不厌（厭）	bǎichībúyàn	v.p.	to never get tired of eating
38. 作东（東）	zuòdōng	v.p.	to be the host (of a dinner)
39. 推辞（辭）	tuīcí	v.	to decline
40. 从命（從）	cóngmìng	v.p.	to obey someone's order

【句型】

一. 难得/難得 *verb phrase*: to be rare; to be hard to come by. This phrase can also be used in the following structures: 1) ... 是很难得的; 2) 难得 + sentence.

    1. 这个机会很难得。

      （這個機會很難得。）

      "Such an opportunity is hard to come by."

    2. 他请大家吃饭是很难得的。

      （他請大家吃飯是很難得的。）

      "It is rare that he invites people to eat."

    3. 难得老板给大家加薪，我们一块儿去吃饭庆祝庆祝吧!

      （難得老板給大家加薪，我們一塊兒去吃飯慶祝慶祝吧!）

      "It is rare for the boss to give us a raise; let's go out to eat and celebrate together."

二. 说的也是/説的也是 *verb phrase*: That is right ...; It is true... This phrase is used to express agreement.

    1. 说的也是，我应该休息了。

      （説的也是，我應該休息了。）

      "You are right, I should have some rest."

    2. 说的也是，他对学生严厉也是为了学生学好。

      （説的也是，他對學生嚴厲也是為了學生學好。）

      "It is true that his strictness with the students is only advantageous to them."

三. 挑得很 *verb phrase*: to be picky/choosy in ... (This phrase is equivalent to 很挑.)

    1. 他吃东西挑得很。

      （他吃東西挑得很。）

      "He is a picky eater."

    2. 他买衣服挑得很。

      （他買衣服挑得很。）

      "He is very picky in buying clothes."

3. 因为他很挑，所以现在还没有找到女朋友。

（因爲他很挑，所以現在還沒有找到女朋友。）

"He is very picky; that is why he still has not found a girlfriend.

四. 恐怕 *verb phrase*: to be afraid that ... (The subject of this verb phrase is normally human beings, and it is often implied but omitted in the sentence.)

1. 现在已经很晚了，恐怕所有的饭馆都关门了。

（現在已經很晚了，恐怕所有的飯館都關門了。）

"It is already very late, and (I) am afraid that all restraurants have closed."

2. 那家餐馆没什么素菜，在那里吃饭恐怕要委屈你了。

（那家餐館沒甚麼素菜，在那裏吃飯恐怕要委屈你了。）

"That restaurant does not have many vegetarian dishes, (I am) afraid that dining there would be inconvenient for you."

3. 我明天有事，恐怕不能去。

（我明天有事，恐怕不能去。）

"I am afraid that I won't be able to go because I have something to do tomorrow."

五. 反而 *adverbial phrase*: contrary to general expectation; on the contrary

1. 很多人都喜欢吃肉，实际上肉吃多了反而没有好处。

（很多人都喜歡吃肉，實際上肉吃多了反而沒有好處。）

"Many people like to eat meat; but in reality, it is to no one's advantage to eat a lot of meat."

2. 人们都说他热情洋溢，他反而不高兴。

（人們都說他熱情洋溢，他反而不高興。）

Everyone says he is full of high spirits. Contrary to everyone's expectation, he was not happy to hear that."

六. 再说/再說 *adverbial phrase*: in addition. This phrase is often used as a connector for listing structures.

1. 他们的菜好吃是好吃，可是太贵，再说他们的菜味精太多。

（他們的菜好吃是好吃，可是太貴，再說他們的菜味精太多。）

"It is true that their dishes are tasty. However, they are too expensive. In addition, they use too much MSG."

2. 那家中国餐馆的菜又好吃又便宜，再说我们还可以在那里练习中文。

（那家中國餐館的菜又好吃又便宜，再說我們還可以在那裏練習中文。）

"The dishes in that Chinese restaurant are not only delicious, but also cheap. In addition, we can also practice our Chinese there."

七. 至于/至於 *preposition*: as for...; The phrase is often used to relate what is currently being discussed with something mentioned in previous discourse.

1. 我明年去中国学习，至于后年我还不知道作什么。

（我明年去中國學習，至於後年我還不知道做甚麼。）

"Next year I am going to study in China. As for the following year, I don't have any plans yet."

2. 他们的饭菜很可口，至于他们的甜点倒是不怎么样。

（他們的飯菜很可口，至於他們的甜點倒是不怎麼樣。）

"Their main dishes are very tasty. As far as their deserts are concerned, they are quite ordinary."

八. 据我（人们）所知（说）/據我（人們）所知（說） *adverbial clause*: As far as I know; It is said ...

1. 据我所知，他虽然有点古怪，但是很善良。

（據我所知，他雖然有點古怪，但是很善良。）

"As far as I know, he is kindhearted, though a bit eccentric."

2. 据人们（所）说，青菜又要涨价了。

（據人們（所）說，青菜又要漲價了。）

"It is said that the price of vegetables is going up again."

3. 据我的同学说，中美关系现在很紧张。

（據我的同學說，中美關係現在很緊張。）

"My classmates said that the relationship between China and the U.S. is very tense."

【语法/語法】

句尾词的用法/句尾詞的用法
(Sentence Final Particles)

In this lesson, we will focus on three particles: 吧、吗, and 呢. All three particles can be used at the end of a sentence, expressing either a question or an assumption, as shown below:

1. 那个问题很难回答吗？ （那個問題很難回答嗎？）

   "Is that question very difficult to answer?"

2. 那个问题很难回答吧？ （那個問題很難回答吧？）

   "That question is very difficult to answer, isn't it?"

3. 哪个问题很难回答呢？ （哪個問題很難回答呢？）

   "Which question is very difficult to answer?"

Students may find it difficult to differentiate among the above three Chinese sentences since they are all interrogatives, the only difference among them being their final particle. The third sentence uses a question word at the beginning of the sentence, whereas the first two do not. Even though these differences are subtle, they are sufficient to express different meanings. The first sentence expresses a pure question; the second sentence expresses the speaker's assumption (i.e., I think the question IS difficult to answer.); and the third sentence shows the speaker's interest in knowing which question is very difficult to answer. It should be noted that it is ungrammatical to say: 那个问题很难回答呢？

Furthermore, the three particles can also be distinctively used to express a progessive situation as in 4, a rhetorical question as in 5, and a suggestion as in 6.

4. 我正吃饭呢！ （我正吃飯呢！） "I am eating now!"

5. 我说的不是很清楚吗？ （我説的不是很清楚嗎？）

   "Wasn't what I said very clear?" (implies: why do you still not understand?)

   5a. 我说的不是很清楚吧？ （我説的不是很清楚吧？）

   "What I said was not very clear, was it?"

6. 中午给自己放个假吧（吗？） （中午給自己放個假吧（嗎？））

   "Why don't you give yourself a break at noon."

Students should be aware that 吗 and 吧 cannot replace 呢 in 4. 吧 sometimes can take the place of 吗 in 5, as shown in 5a; however, the meaning of the two sentences changed accordingly, as shown by the English translation. Both 吧 and 吗 can express a suggestion as in 6, but 呢 does not have this function.

【补充词汇/補充詞彙】

排队 （隊）	páiduì	v.	to line up
刷卡	shuākǎ	v.	to scan a card
密码 （碼）	mìmǎ	n.	code, password
菜单 （單）	càidān	n.	menu
餐具	cānjù	n.	tableware
刀子	dāozi	n.	knife
叉子	chāzi	n.	fork
筷子	kuàizi	n.	chopsticks
盘子 （盤）	pánzi	n.	plate
汤匙 （湯）	tāngchí	n.	spoon
碗	wǎn	n.	bowl
肉	ròu	n.	meat
火腿 （腿）	huǒtuǐ	n.	ham
香肠 （腸）	xiāngcháng	n.	sausage
牛肉	niúròu	n.	beef
牛排	niúpái	n.	steak
猪肉	zhūròu	n.	pork
猪排	zhūpái	n.	pork chops
羊肉	yángròu	n.	lamb (meat)
鸡 （鷄）	jī	n.	chicken
老	lǎo	adj.	(to be) tough, overdone
嫩	nèn	adj.	(to be) tender
龙吓 （龍蝦）	lóngxiā	n.	lobster
蔬菜	shūcài	n.	vegetable
茄子	qiézi	n.	eggplant
黄瓜 （黃）	huángguā	n.	cucumber
葱	cōng	n.	green onion (scallion)
蒜	suàn	n.	garlic

姜（薑）	jiāng	n.	ginger
面条（麵條）	miàntiáo	n.	noodle
面包（麵）	miànbāo	n.	bread
三明治	sānmíngzhì	n.	sandwich
水果	shuǐguǒ	n.	fruit
苹果（蘋）	píngguǒ	n.	apple
桔子（橘）	júzi	n.	orange
樱桃（櫻）	yīngtáo	n.	cherry
草莓	cǎoméi	n.	strawberry
葡萄	pútao	n.	grapes
葡萄干（乾）	pútaogān	n.	raisins
柠檬（檸）	níngméng	n.	lemon
香蕉	xiāngjiāo	n.	banana
西瓜	xīguā	n.	watermelon
饮料（飲）	yǐnliào	n.	drink
汽水	qìshuǐ	n.	soda
啤酒	píjiǔ	n.	beer
果酱（醬）	guǒjiàng	n.	jelly
花生酱（醬）	huāshēng jiàng	n.	peanut butter
奶油	nǎiyóu	n.	butter
奶酪	nǎilào	n.	cheese
甜点（點）	tiándiǎn	n.	dessert
蛋糕	dàngāo	n.	(egg) cake
冰淇淋	bīngqílín	n.	ice cream
胡椒	hújiāo	n.	pepper
辣椒	làjiāo	n.	hot pepper
醋	cù	n.	vinegar
盐（鹽）	yán	n.	salt

【练习】

一. 用指定的词回答问题：

　　1. 请你谈谈李小姐的饮食习惯。 （挑得很，吃素，至于）

　　2. 王先生和李小姐的饮食习惯有什么不同？ （至于，之所以...是因为...）

　　3. 王先生和李小姐为什么决定去江浙菜馆？ （百吃不厌，免费，特别）

　　4. 你觉得吃素好还是吃肉好？为什么？ （反而，再说，据我所知）

二. 造句：

　　1. 据我所知

　　2. 之所以...是因为

　　3. 谁也别...

4. 难得

5. 反而

三. 填空（有的词可以用多次）：

作东、说的也是、吧、直言不讳、挑得很、呢、推辞、
精致、新鲜

A: 我们一星期都这么忙，今天是星期五，我们一起去吃晚饭＿＿＿＿！

B: ＿＿＿＿＿＿＿＿＿，王先生呢？今天该轮到我们＿＿＿＿＿＿＿＿＿＿请他了。

A: 他正在打电话＿＿＿＿＿＿！他那个人客气得很，希望他不会＿＿＿＿＿＿＿＿。

B: 今天我们去哪吃＿＿＿＿＿＿？你选＿＿＿＿＿＿。

A: 那我就＿＿＿＿＿＿了。不过，我们还是等王先生来了再决定吧！他吃
东西＿＿＿＿＿＿。

B. 我倒想起一家饭馆，他们的东西很＿＿＿＿＿＿，菜做得很＿＿＿＿＿＿＿，再
说价钱也不贵。

A: 好＿＿＿＿＿＿！我们就决定去那儿。

四. 作文：谈谈你最喜欢的一家餐馆(100字以上)(You may find the following
structures helpful:

1. Listing Structure: 不但 …而且 … 再说 …

2. Comparison with supporting opinions: …比 … , 比方说 …

【練習】

一. 用指定的詞回答問題：

　1. 請你談談李小姐的飲食習慣。　〔挑得很，吃素，至於〕

　2. 王先生和李小姐的飲食習慣有甚麼不同？　〔至於，之所以...是因為...〕

　3. 王先生和李小姐為甚麼決定去江浙菜館？　〔百吃不厭，免費，特別〕

　4. 你覺得吃素好還是吃肉好？為甚麼？　〔反而，再說，據我所知〕

二. 造句：

　1. 據我所知

　2. 之所以...是因為

　3. 誰也別...

4. 難得

5. 反而

三. 填空（有的辭可以用多次）：

作東、説的也是、吧、直言不諱、挑得很、呢、推辭、
精致、新鮮

A: 我們一星期都這麼忙，今天是星期五，我們一起去吃晚飯＿＿＿＿！

B: ＿＿＿＿＿＿＿＿＿，王先生呢？今天該輪到我們＿＿＿＿＿＿＿＿＿＿請他了。

A: 他正在打電話＿＿＿＿＿＿！他那個人客氣得很，希望他不會＿＿＿＿＿＿＿＿。

B: 今天我們去哪吃＿＿＿＿＿＿？你選＿＿＿＿＿＿。

A: 那我就＿＿＿＿＿＿了。不過，我們還是等王先生來了再決定吧！他吃
東西＿＿＿＿＿＿。

B. 我倒想起一家飯館，他們的東西很＿＿＿＿＿＿，菜做得很＿＿＿＿＿＿＿，再
説價錢也不貴。

A: 好＿＿＿＿＿＿！我們就決定去那兒。

四. 作文：談談你最喜歡的一家餐館(100字以上; you may find the following
structures helpful)：

1. Listing Structure: 不但 ...而且 ... 再説 ...

2. Comparison with supporting opinions: ...比 ... , 比方説 ...

【衍生活动】
解决难题

你请了五位客人去餐馆吃饭，在他们当中有一位是素食主义者，有一位是七十岁的老先生，现在请你开出最合适的菜单。你在课前至少要读懂十五道菜名，然后在课堂上说明你为什么选这些菜。

菜单：

鱼香肉丝	鱼香茄子	麻婆豆腐
素三鲜	酸辣白菜	葱油饼
葱油鸡	蕃茄排骨汤	香菇炖鸡
糖醋鱼	宫保鸡丁	牛肉蒸饺
凉拌黄瓜	凤梨炒牛肉	青豆虾仁
干煸四季豆	红烧肉	炸虾球
干贝生菜	豆芽鸡丝	蚝油西兰花
中式牛排	素包子	葱爆里肌
沙锅鱼头	豆沙粽子	豆瓣鱼

【衍生活動】

解決難題

你請了五位客人去餐館吃飯，在他們當中有一位是素食主義者，有一位是七十歲的老先生，現在請你開出最合適的菜單。你在課前至少要讀懂十五道菜名，然後在課堂上說明你為甚麼選這些菜。

菜單：

魚香肉絲	魚香茄子	麻婆豆腐
素三鮮	酸辣白菜	蔥油餅
蔥油雞	蕃茄排骨湯	香菇燉雞
糖醋魚	宮保雞丁	牛肉蒸餃
涼拌黃瓜	鳳梨炒牛肉	青豆蝦仁
乾煸四季豆	紅燒肉	炸蝦球
干貝生菜	豆芽雞絲	蠔油西蘭花
中式牛排	素包子	蔥爆裹肌
沙鍋魚頭	豆沙粽子	豆瓣魚

【第七課】

音樂欣賞

【课文】

音乐欣赏

甲： 我热爱音乐，要是生活中没有音乐，我就会像一滩死水失去了活力。

乙： 我也喜欢音乐，不过没有音乐，我仍然可以照常工作、过日子。在我的生活中，音乐只能算是配角。就是有一天音乐从这个世界上消失了，我也能找到其他的寄托，让自己过得愉快。我把音乐当成一个好朋友，好朋友离开了，可以再交新的朋友，不是吗？

甲： 我很羡慕你的理智和洒脱。对我来说，音乐不仅仅是一个朋友，而是我所有的朋友，音乐能解除身体的疲倦和内心的烦恼，而且可以帮助我认识生活的美好。

乙： 我不太懂音乐，也没有时间仔细欣赏音乐，但是我也知道有的音乐听上去很轻松自在，有的却让人感到烦躁不安，比如像摇滚乐。

甲： 看来你是喜欢古典音乐。你喜欢谁的曲子呢？

乙： 有时候听听莫扎特的小夜曲和弦乐四重奏，其它的就听得很少了。你既然懂音乐，能不能给我推荐一些值得细细品味的名曲？

甲： 你可以听听舒伯特，史特劳斯，柴可夫斯基等作曲家的交响曲和圆舞曲。他们都是一流的古典音乐作曲家。

乙： 我也喜欢钢琴曲。小的时候学过一点儿钢琴，但后来就很少摸了。

甲： 人们都说萧邦的钢琴曲天下第一，不过，我倒是更喜欢舒曼的钢琴曲。

乙： 这么说你也喜欢钢琴曲？

甲： 不仅仅是钢琴曲，实际上我对什么音乐都感兴趣，从古典音乐到爵士乐，从民乐到流行音乐，没有我不喜欢的。这些音乐各有各的风格，各有各的特点。不同的音乐给人的感受也不同。譬如，古典音乐给人一种高雅、浪漫、雄壮、浑然忘我的感觉。民歌呢，充满了乡土气息，使人感到故乡生活的美好。而流行歌曲往往反映了现代人的意识形态。

乙： 照你这么说，什么音乐我都应该听听？！

甲： 是的，而且无论什么时候听对你都有帮助：高兴的时候听，你会更高兴；不高兴的时候听，你会忘掉不高兴的事；有压力的时候听，你会慢慢地轻松起来。

乙： 的确，你对音乐懂得很多，可称得上是音乐通了。

甲： 你千万别这么说。我只是有兴趣而已。

乙： 听音乐既然有那么多好处，我今后一定要时常听听音乐。

讨论题：
1. 国家为什么要有国歌？
2. 音乐能不能超越国界？能不能超越时间？
3. 有的人认为现代的音乐不算艺术，你认为呢？
4. 音乐对生活到底有什么影响？
5. 如果这个世界上没有音乐，你的生活会有什么不同？
6. 你喜欢什么音乐？为什么？

【課文】

音樂欣賞

甲：　我熱愛音樂，要是生活中沒有音樂，我就會像一灘死水失去了活力。

乙：　我也喜歡音樂，不過沒有音樂，我仍然可以照常工作，過日子。在我的生活中，音樂只能算是配角。就是有一天音樂從這個世界上消失了，我也能找到其他的寄托，讓自己過得愉快。我把音樂當成一個好朋友，好朋友離開了，可以再交新的朋友，不是嗎？

甲：　我很羨慕你的理智和灑脫。對我來說，音樂不僅僅是一個朋友，而是我所有的朋友，音樂能解除身體的疲倦和內心的煩惱，而且可以幫助我認識生活的美好。

乙：　我不太懂音樂，也沒有時間仔細欣賞音樂，但是我也知道有的音樂聽上去很輕鬆自在，有的卻讓人感到煩躁不安，比如像搖滾樂。

甲：　看來你是喜歡古典音樂。你喜歡誰的曲子呢？

乙：　有時候聽聽莫扎特的小夜曲和弦樂四重奏，其它的就聽得很少了。你既然懂音樂，能不能給我推薦一些值得細細品味的名曲？

甲：　你可以聽聽舒伯特，史特勞斯，柴可夫斯基等作曲家的交響曲和圓舞曲。他們都是一流的古典音樂作曲家。

乙： 我也喜歡鋼琴曲。小的時候學過一點兒鋼琴，但後來就很少摸了。

甲： 人們都說蕭邦的鋼琴曲天下第一，不過，我倒是更喜歡舒曼的鋼琴曲。

乙： 這麼說你也喜歡鋼琴曲？

甲： 不僅僅是鋼琴曲，實際上我對什麼音樂都感興趣，從古典音樂到爵士樂，從民樂到流行音樂，沒有我不喜歡的。這些音樂各有各的風格，各有各的特點。不同的音樂給人的感受也不同。譬如，古典音樂給人一種高雅、浪漫、雄壯、渾然忘我的感覺。民歌呢，充滿了鄉土氣息，使人感到故鄉生活的美好。而流行歌曲往往反映了現代人的意識形態。

乙： 照你這麼說，甚麼音樂我都應該聽聽？！

甲： 是的，而且無論甚麼時候聽對你都有幫助：高興的時候聽，你會更高興；不高興的時候聽，你會忘掉不高興的事；有壓力的時候聽，你會慢慢地輕鬆起來。

乙： 的確，你對音樂懂得很多，可稱得上是音樂通了。

甲： 你千萬別這麼說。我只是有興趣而已。

乙： 聽音樂既然有那麼多好處，我今後一定要時常聽聽。

討論題：
1. 國家為甚麼要有國歌？
2. 音樂能不能超越國界？能不能超越時間？
3. 有的人認為現代的音樂不算藝術，你認為呢？
4. 音樂對生活到底有甚麼影響？
5. 如果這個世界上沒有音樂，你的生活會有甚麼不同？
6. 你喜歡甚麼音樂？為甚麼？

【生词/生詞】

1. 欣赏 （赏）	xīnshǎng	v.	to enjoy, to appreciate
2. 热爱 （熱愛）	rè'ài	v.	to love ardently
3. 失去	shīqù	v.	to lose
4. 一滩 （灘）	yītān	cl.	measure word for liquid
5. 活力	huólì	n.	vitality
6. 配角	pèijué	n.	supporting role
7. 消失	xiāoshī	v.	to disappear
8. 寄托	jìtuō	n./v.	placing (hopes, etc) on; to place hope(s) on
9. 羡慕	xiànmù	v.	to envy, to admire
10. 理智	lǐzhì	n./adj.	reason, intellect; (to be) reasonable
11. 洒脱 （灑）	sǎtuō	v	to be free and easy in style
12. 解除	jiěchú	v.	to remove
13. 疲倦	píjuàn	n./adj.	fatigue; (to be) tired
14. 烦恼 （煩惱）	fánnǎo	n./adj.	agitation; (to be) agitated
15. 仔细 （細）	zǐxì	adj.	(to be) careful, attentive
16. 烦躁不安 （煩）	fánzàobù'ān	v.p.	to be annoyed
17. 摇滚乐 （樂）	yáogǔnyuè	n.	rock and roll
18. 古典	gǔdiǎn	adj.	(to be) classical
19. 曲子	qǔzi	n.	music
20. 莫扎特	mòzhātè	N.	Mozart
21. 小夜曲	xiǎoyèqǔ	n.	serenade
22. 弦乐 （樂）	xiányuè	n.	string music
23. 四重奏	sìchóngzòu	n.	quartet
24. 推荐 （薦）	tuījiàn	v.	to recommend
25. 细细 （細細）	xìxì	adj./adv	careful; carefully
26. 品味	pǐnwèi	v.	to taste, to savor

27. 舒伯特	shūbótè	N.	Schubert
28. 史特劳斯（劳）	shǐtèláosī	N	Strauss
29. 柴可夫斯基	cháikěfūsījī	N.	Tchaikovsky
30. 作曲家	zuòqǔjiā	n.p.	composer
31. 交响曲（響）	jiāoxiǎngqǔ	n.	symphony
32. 圆舞曲（圆）	yuánwǔqǔ	n.	waltz
33. 钢琴曲（鋼）	gāngqínqǔ	n.	piano concerto
34. 摸	mō	v.	to touch
35. 萧邦（蕭）	xiāobāng	N.	Chopin
36. 天下	tiānxià	adv./n.	in the world; the world
37. 舒曼	shūmàn	N.	Schumann
38. 爵士乐（樂）	juéshìyuè	n.	jazz
39. 民乐（樂）	mínyuè	n.	folk music
40. 流行	liúxíng	adj.	(to be) popular
41. 风格（風）	fēnggé	n.	style
42. 特点（點）	tèdiǎn	n.	characteristic
43. 高雅	gāoyǎ	adj.	(to be) noble and elegant
44. 浪漫	làngmàn	adj.	(to be) romantic
45. 雄壮（壯）	xióngzhuàng	adj.	(to be) magnificent
46. 浑然忘我（渾）	húnránwàngwǒ	v.p.	to be totally involved
47. 充满	chōngmǎn	v.	to be full of
48. 乡土（鄉）	xiāngtǔ	n.	countryside
49. 气息（氣）	qìxī	n.	flavor
50. 反映	fǎnyìng	v.	to reflect
51. 意识形态（識、態）	yìshìxíngtài	n.p.	ideology
52. 称得上（稱）	chēngdeshàng	v.p.	can be considered
53. 音乐通（樂）	yīnyuètōng	n.p.	expert in music
54. 超越	chāoyuè	v.	to surpass
55. 艺术（藝術）	yìshù	n.	art

【句型】

一. 看来/看來... *verb phrase*: It seems that ..., to look ...

    1. 看来我得好好用功，要不然我一定考不好。

      （看來我得好好用功，要不然我一定考不好。）

       "It seems that I have to study hard; otherwise, I definitely cannot do well on the exam."

    2. 看来美国的经济不会一下好转。

      （看來美國的經濟不會一下好轉。）

       "It seems as if the American economy will not improve for a while."

    3. 他们俩关系那么好，看来他们很快就要结婚了。

      （他們倆關係那麼好，看來他們很快就要結婚了。）

       "They have been getting along with each other very well. It looks as though they are going to get married soon."

二. 人们都说/人們都說... *subject + verb phrase*: People say..., It is said that...

    1. 人们都说中国有很多值得参观的地方。

      （人們都説中國有很多值得參觀的地方。）

       "Everyone says that there are a lot of places in China which are worthwhile to visit."

    2. 人们都说所有的汽车都要涨价了。

      （人們都説所有的汽車都要漲價了。）

       "It is said that the prices of all automobiles are going up."

三. 从...到/從...到... *prepositional phrase*: from ... to ...

    1. 从北京到天津，坐火车要三个小时。

      （從北京到天津，坐火車要三個小時。）

       "It takes three hours by train from Beijing to Tianjin."

    2. 从长篇小说到短篇故事，他都喜欢看。

      （從長篇小説到短篇故事，他都喜歡看。）

       "He likes to read everything from novels to short stories."

3. 从他祖父到他，三代人都是教书的。

(從他祖父到他，三代人都是教書的。)

"The three generations from his grandfather to him are all teachers."

四. 充满/充滿 *verb phrase*: to be full of...

1. 这个房子里充满了臭气。

(這個房子裏充滿了臭氣。)

"This house is full of bad fumes."

2. 大多数年轻人对生活充满了信心。

(大多數年輕人對生活充滿了信心。)

"Most young people have full confidence in life."

3. 教室里充满了学生的欢声笑语。

(教室裏充滿了學生的歡聲笑語。)

"The classroom is full of students' laughter."

五. 照...这么+S/照...這麼+S; *preposition + S:* according to what one says, does, etc...; if one does...like this, ...

1. 照他这么说，我们没有办法解决这个问题。

(照他這麼説，我們沒有辦法解決這個問題。)

"According to what he said, there is no way for us to solve the problem."

2. 照他这么花钱，很快就会变成穷光蛋。

(照他這麼花錢，很快就會變成窮光蛋。)

"If he spends his money like this, he will soon become a poor wretch."

3. 照他们这么写文章，没有人能看得懂。

(照他們這麼寫文章，沒有人能看得懂。)

"If he writes articles this way, no one will understand them."

【语法/語法】

否定式
(Negation)

There are three negative markers which are most often used in modern Chinese: 不、别、没. All three markers occur in the text of this lesson. Following are more examples:

1. 教室里没〔有〕灯光。/教室裏沒〔有〕燈光。

   "There is no light in the classroom."

2. 我没〔有〕很多钱。/我沒〔有〕很多錢。

   "I don't have a lot of money."

3. 他不是我找的那个人。/他不是我找的那個人。

   "He is not the one for whom I am looking."

4. 我不知道中文这么容易学。/我不知道中文這麼容易學。

   "I did not know that it is so easy to study Chinese."

5. 你去图书馆，别忘了给我借那本书。

   （你去圖書館，別忘了給我借那本書。）

   "Don't forget to borrow that book for me when you go to the library."

In general, 没 is used when the verb is 有, expressing existence or possession, as exemplified in sentences 1 and 2. Notice that 有 in these cases can be omitted. When the verb is stative such as 是 or 知道 in sentences 3 and 4, 不 is used. If the sentences are imperative as 5, 别 is used. These are the clear cases. There are also a great number of verbs which do not belong to any type discussed above. These verbs can be negated by either 不 or 没 depending upon whether the sentence describes a fact or a completion of an action. Consider the following examples:

6. 他不写作业。/他不寫作業。

   "He does not do (or is not doing) his homework.

7. 他没〔有〕写作业。/他沒〔有〕寫作業。

   "He has not done his homework."

Sentence 6 states the fact that he does not do his homework, while sentence 7 describes that the event (writing his homework) has not yet been completed. In addition to this, students should also pay attention to the position of the negative markers.

    8. 我不一定去看电影。/我不一定去看電影。

      "I am not sure whether I am going to the movie."

    9. 我一定不去看电影。/我一定不去看電影。

      "I am definitely not going to see the movie."

Notice that the different positions of 不 in 8 and 9 create quite different meanings for the two sentences. In 8, 不 negates "definitely", while in 9, it negates the verb "go".

【补充词汇/補充詞彙】

音乐会 （樂會）	yīnyuèhuì	n.	concert
协奏曲 （协）	xiézòuqǔ	n.	concerto
奏鸣曲 （鳴）	zòumíngqǔ	n.	sonata
室内乐 （樂）	shìnèiyuè	n.	chamber music
国乐 （國樂）	guóyuè	n.	Chinese classical music
歌剧 （劇）	gējù	n.	opera
民谣 （謠）	mínyáo	n.	folk music
国歌 （國）	guógē	n.	national anthem
音响 （響）	yīnxiǎng	n.	stereo system
杂音 （雜音）	záyīn	n.	noise
乐团 （樂團）	yuètuán	n.	orchestra
合唱团 （團）	héchàngtuán	n.	chorus
小提琴	xiǎotíqín	n.	violin
长笛 （長）	chángdí	n.	flute
吉他	jítā	n.	guitar
鼓	gǔ	n.	drums

喇叭	lǎbā	n.	trumpet
乐谱 (樂譜)	yuèpǔ	n.	sheet music
指挥 (揮)	zhǐhuī	v./n.	to conduct; conductor
大调 (調)	dàdiào	n.	major
小调 (調)	xiǎodiào	n.	minor
拉	lā	v.	to play (violin)
弹 (彈)	tán	v.	to play (guitar, piano)
吹	chuī	v.	to play (trumpet, flute)
打	dǎ	v.	to play (drums)
演奏	yǎnzòu	v./n.	to perform; performance
伴奏	bànzòu	v./n.	to accompany; accompaniment
合唱	héchàng	v./n.	to sing in unison; singing in unison
独唱 (獨)	dúchàng	v./n.	to sing solo; solo (vocal)
独奏 (獨)	dúzòu	v./n.	to play a solo; solo (instrument)
节奏 (節)	jiézòu	n.	rhythm
唱片	chàngpiàn	n.	record
镭射唱片	léishèchàngpiàn	n.	laser disc
耳机 (機)	ěrjī	n.	earphones
鼓掌	gǔzhǎng	v./n.	to applaud; applause
喝彩	hècǎi	v./n.	to cheer; cheer
甜美	tiánměi	adj.	(to be) sweet
刺激	cìjī	v.	to be stimulating
陶醉	táozuì	v.	to be intoxicated, to be overwhelmed

【练习】

一. 完成句子:

1. 就是不高兴的时候，他 _____。

2. 照他那么说，什么人都 _____。

3. 无论什么时候 _____。

4. 不同的音乐给人的感受不同，比方说，_____。

5. 人们都说 _____。

二. 造句:

1. 看来

2. 烦躁不安

3. 充满

4. 从... 到...

5. 称得上

三. 用所给的词语完成下面的对话：

> 烦躁不安、解除、品味、称得上、天下第一、
> 欣赏、推荐、倒是、别、不、没

甲：我听的古典音乐_____多。你能_____能给我_____一些有名的
　　西洋古典音乐？

乙：依我看，史特劳斯的圆舞曲可以_____是最流行的古典音乐。

甲：我很少听圆舞曲，我比较_____钢琴曲。

乙：我同意，特别是当我_____的时候，钢琴曲最能_____我的烦恼。

甲：人们都说萧邦的钢琴曲_____，你同意吗？

乙：我说实话，你可_____生气。我不喜欢他的钢琴曲，我比较喜欢贝
　　多芬的。

甲：我想喜欢哪位作曲家并_____重要。只要我们细细_____，就会明
　　白这些音乐各有各的风格，各有各的特点。

乙：我从来_____听过中国的民乐曲。你听过吗？

甲：听过，很有意思。有机会，你也应该听听。

四. 作文题：为什么一个国家要有国歌？

【練習】

一. 完成句子：

    1. 就是不高興的時候他 _____。

    2. 照他那麼說，甚麼人都 _____。

    3. 無論甚麼時候 _____。

    4. 不同的音樂給人的感受不同，比方說，_____。

    5. 人們都說 _____。

二. 造句：

    1. 看來

    2. 煩躁不安

    3. 充滿

    4. 從... 到...

    5. 稱得上

三. 用所給的詞語完成下面的對話：

　　　　煩躁不安、解除、品味、稱得上、天下第一、
　　　　欣賞、推薦、倒是、別、不、沒

甲：我聽的古典音樂_____多。你能_____能給我_____一些有名的
　　西洋古典音樂？
乙：依我看，史特勞斯的圓舞曲可以_____是最流行的古典音樂。
甲：我很少聽圓舞曲，我比較_____鋼琴曲。
乙：我同意，特別是當我_____的時候，鋼琴曲最能_____我的煩惱。
甲：人們都說蕭邦的鋼琴曲_____，你同意嗎？
乙：我說實話，你可_____生氣。我不喜歡他的鋼琴曲，我比較喜歡貝
　　多芬的。
甲：我想喜歡哪位作曲家並_____重要。只要我們細細_____，就會明
　　白這些音樂各有各的風格，各有各的特點。
乙：我從來_____聽過中國的民樂曲。你聽過嗎？
甲：聽過，很有意思。有機會，你也應該聽聽。

四. 作文題：爲甚麼一個國家要有國歌？

【衍生活动】

标点与翻译

请将以下短文标上标点并翻译成你的母语（参考标点符号：，。、？：「」）：

我的好朋友

如果有人问你最好的朋友是谁我的回答大概是贝多芬（BEETHOVEN）第九交响曲（SYMPHONY）的第三乐章(MOVEMENT) 可能你觉得这个回答有一点儿奇怪好朋友为什么会是一首曲子而不是人不过只要你仔细想想就能了解我为什么这么说假如你的好朋友是一个人你们之间就一定有距离也就是说人不可能会完全了解另外一个人因为各人有各人的经验强迫自己去了解别人或是勉强别人来了解自己都是不自然的行为NO.9的第三乐章为什么是我的好朋友是从什么时候开始的我也不太清楚只是每当我痛苦的时候就会想一再地听它听了几次心情就好多了特别是秋天的黄昏坐在河边一面吹著凉风看夕阳一面听这首曲子人世间所有的问题就都不存在了我们也可以从这首曲子中看到老年贝多芬对世界的看法是既浪漫又充满了深刻的爱

【衍生活動】

標點與翻譯

請將以下短文標上標點並翻譯成你的母語（參考標點符號： ， 。 、 ？ ：
「」）：

我的好朋友

如果有人問你最好的朋友是誰我的回答大概是貝多芬（BEETHOVEN）第九交響曲（SYMPHONY）的第三樂章（MOVEMENT）可能你覺得這個回答有一點兒奇怪好朋友為甚麼會是一首曲子而不是人不過只要你仔細想想就能了解我為甚麼這麼說假如你的好朋友是一個人你們之間就一定有距離也就是說人不可能會完全了解另外一個人因為各人有各人的經驗強迫自己去了解別人或是勉強別人來了解自己都是不自然的行為NO.9的第三樂章為甚麼是我的好朋友是從甚麼時候開始的我也不太清楚只是每當我痛苦的時候就會想一再地聽它聽了幾次心情就好多了特別是秋天的黃昏坐在河邊一面吹著涼風看夕陽一面聽這首曲子人世間所有的問題就都不存在了我們也可以從這首曲子中看到老年貝多芬對世界的看法是既浪漫又充滿了深刻的愛

【第八課】

他有罪嗎？

【课文】

他有罪吗？

王建国是位资深警官，在警界服务达二十年，抓了不少毒贩。他万万沒想到，在退休前夕，自己竟成了法庭上的被告。今天，他得面对陪审团说明一切…

法官： 有人检举，说你为了提高自己的工作效率，让警犬染上毒瘾，五年来，已经有十几条警犬受到伤害，你为什么这样做呢？

警官： 这是不得已的。您知道，缉毒可不容易，我们要靠狗灵敏的嗅觉。可是，训练一条狗去辨识毒品的味道要两年，得花五万块美金。这笔钱不是小数目。最近，经济不景气，警局的预算一再被削减。老实说，从五年前开始，我们就付不起训练费用了。为了缉毒，只好让狗染上毒瘾。

法官： 这是你自己的主意吗？请你把过程交代清楚。

警官： 当时，为了警犬的训练费，我伤透了脑筋，最后只好去找养狗专家。他给了我一套既省时又省钱的办法，就是每餐把少量的毒品搀在狗食中，不到三个月，警犬就会染上毒瘾，有了毒瘾之后，警犬就可以开始协助缉毒了。平常，我们在机场的检查站工作，分早、晚两班。早班的警犬在前一天晚上，不喂毒品，等它毒瘾发作的时候，自然就会特别注意毒品的味道。

法官： 你身为执法人员，怎么能知法犯法呢？

警官： 我查过，以往并没有类似的案例。我想一定会有人说我「虐待」动物或是不人道什么的。不过，每天也有不少白老鼠在实验室里丧命，还有更多的牛、羊、猪进了人的肚子。法庭上要是真的判我有罪，我会上诉到底，这对我不公平。

法官： 我很了解你的心情，不过狗是人类最忠实的朋友，人对狗的感情跟对别的动物是不一样的。你利用了朋友。

警官： 法官大人，我真希望你能去看看那些染上了毒瘾的狗，那样你才能真的了解我此刻的心情。狗会不顾一切地去找毒品，人不也是一样？为了毒品干会尽所有的坏事：勒索、卖春、偷窃，甚至杀人、抢银行。我不是不爱狗，只是我更在乎人。

讨论题：

1. 请你替法官说完这段话。
2. 如果你是陪审团的一员，你会判警官有罪吗？为什么？

【課文】

他有罪嗎？

王建國是位資深警官，在警界服務達二十年，抓了不少毒販。他萬萬沒想到，在退休前夕，自己竟成了法庭上的被告。今天，他得面對陪審團說明一切…

法官： 有人檢舉，說你為了提高自己的工作效率，讓警犬染上毒癮，五年來，已經有十幾條警犬受到傷害，你為甚麼這樣做呢？

警官： 這是不得已的。您知道，緝毒可不容易，我們要靠狗靈敏的嗅覺。可是，訓練一條狗去辨識毒品的味道要兩年，得花五萬塊美金。這筆錢不是小數目。最近，經濟不景氣，警局的預算一再被削減。老實說，從五年前開始，我們就付不起訓練費用了。為了緝毒，只好讓狗染上毒癮。

法官： 這是你自己的主意嗎？請你把過程交代清楚。

警官： 當時，為了警犬的訓練費，我傷透了腦筋，最後只好去找養狗專家。他給了我一套既省時又省錢的辦法，就是每餐把少量的毒品攪在狗食中，不到三個月，警犬就會染上毒癮，有了毒癮之後，警犬就可以開始協助緝毒了。平常，我們在機場的檢查站工作，分早、晚兩班。早班

的警犬在前一天晚上，不餵毒品，等牠毒癮發作的時候，
自然就會特別注意毒品的味道。

法官：你身為執法人員，怎麼能知法犯法呢？

警官：我查過，以往並沒有類似的案例。我想一定會有人說我
「虐待」動物或是不人道甚麼的。不過，每天也有不少
白老鼠在實驗室裡喪命，還有更多的牛、羊、豬進了人
的肚子。法庭上要是真的判我有罪，我會上訴到底，這
對我不公平。

法官：我很了解你的心情，不過狗是人類最忠實的朋友，人對
狗的感情跟對別的動物是不一樣的。你利用了朋友。

警官：法官大人，我真希望你能去看看那些染上了毒癮的狗，
那樣你才能真的了解我此刻的心情。狗會不顧一切地去
找毒品，人不也是一樣？為了毒品會幹盡所有的壞事：
勒索、賣春、偷竊，甚至殺人、搶銀行。我不是不愛狗，
只是我更在乎人。

討論題：
  1. 請你替法官說完這段話。
  2. 如果你是陪審團的一員，你會判警官有罪嗎？為甚麼？

【生词/生詞】

1. 有罪	yǒuzuì	v.p.	guilty (of a crime)
2. 资深 （資）	zīshēn	adj.	(to be) experienced
3. 警官	jǐngguān	n.	police officer
4. 警界	jǐngjiè	n.	the police profession
5. 毒贩 （販）	dúfàn	n.	drug dealer
6. 退休	tuìxiū	v.	to retire
7. 前夕	qiánxī	adv.	the time before...
8. 法庭	fǎtíng	n.	court
9. 被告	bèigào	n.	defendant
10. 面对 （對）	miànduì	v.	to face
11. 陪审团 （審團）	péishěntuán	n.	jury
12. 检举 （檢舉）	jiǎnjǔ	v.	to report (a legal offender)
13. 提高	tígāo	v.	to raise, to increase
14. 效率	xiàolǜ	n.	efficiency
15. 警犬	jǐngquǎn	n.	police dog
16. 染上	rǎnshàng	v.	to get addicted to
17. 毒瘾 （瘾）	dúyǐn	n.	drug addiction
18. 缉毒 （緝）	jìdú	v.	to apprehend drug dealers
19. 灵敏 （靈）	língmǐn	adj.	(to be) sensitive
20. 嗅觉 （覺）	xiùjué	n.	sense of smell
21. 训练 （訓練）	xùnliàn	v./n.	to train; training
22. 辨识 （識）	biànshí	v.	to distinguish, to identify
23. 毒品	dúpǐn	n.	drugs
24. 味道	wèidào	n.	smell, taste
25. 景气 （氣）	jǐngqì	adj.	(to be) prosperous
26. 预算 （預）	yùsuàn	n.	budget
27. 削减	xiāojiǎn	v.	to reduce

28. 老实说〔實〕	lǎoshíshuō v.p.		honestly speaking
29. 费用〔費〕	fèiyòng	n.	expense
30. 过程〔過〕	guòchéng	n.	process
31. 交代	jiāodài	v.	to explain (unwillingly)
32. 伤透〔傷〕	shāngtòu	v.	to be bothersome
33. 脑筋〔腦〕	nǎojīn	n.	mind
34. 专家〔專〕	zhuānjiā	n.	expert
35. 搀〔攙〕	chān	v.	to mix
36. 协助〔協〕	xiézhù	v.	to assist
37. 喂〔餵〕	wèi	v.	to feed
38. 发作〔發〕	fāzuò	v.	(of addiction, disease) to start
39. 执法〔執〕	zhífǎ	v.p.	to enforce the law
40. 犯法	fànfǎ	v.p.	to commit a crime
41. 查	chá	v.	to check, to examine
42. 类似〔類〕	lèisì	adj.	(to be) similar
43. 案例	ànlì	n.	precedent (of criminal investigation)
44. 虐待	nüèdài	v.	to abuse
45. 不人道	bù réndào	v.p.	inhumane
46. 白老鼠	báilǎoshǔ	n.p.	guinea pig
47. 实验〔實驗〕	shíyàn	n.	to experiment
48. 丧命〔喪〕	sàngmìng	v.p.	to lose one's life
49. 上诉〔訴〕	shàngsù	v.	to appeal (legal term)
50. 公平	gōngpíng	adj.	(to be) fair
51. 忠实〔實〕	zhōngshí	adj.	(to be) loyal
52. 勒索	lèsuǒ	v.	to blackmail
53. 卖春〔賣〕	màichūn	v.	to be a prostitute
54. 偷窃〔竊〕	tōuqiè	v.	to steal
55. 抢〔搶〕	qiǎng	v.	to rob

【句型】

一. 达/達... *verb*: to amount to

　　1. 他在警界服务达二十年之久。

　　　　（他在警界服務達二十年之久。）

　　　"He served on the police force for as long as 20 years. "

　　2. 到目前为止，这个国家的贸易逆差达三十亿美元。

　　　　（到目前為止，這個國家的貿易逆差達三十億美元。）

　　　"As of now, the trade deficit of this country has reached $3 billion."

二. 万万/萬萬 *adverb*: absolutely; This is used before a word of negation.

　　1. 我万万没有想到她会杀人。

　　　　（我萬萬沒有想到她會殺人。）

　　　"I never thought that she would kill someone."

　　2. 你万万不能作对不起父母的事。

　　　　（你萬萬不能作對不起父母的事。）

　　　"You should never, ever do something that would let your parents down."

三. 付不起/付不起 *verb phrase*: cannot afford to pay... There are many other similar structures, such as 买不起, 看不起(someone), 负不起(responsibility).

　　1. 谁也付不起这种价钱。

　　　　（誰也付不起這種價錢。）

　　　"Nobody can afford this kind of price."

　　2. 如果你负不起这种责任，就别作这件事。

　　　　（如果你負不起這種責任，就別作這件事。）

　　　"If you cannot afford to take responsibility, then do not do this."

四. 老实说/老實説 *adverbial phrase*: honestly speaking

　　1. 老实说，我的钱已经用完了。

　　　　（老實説，我的錢已經用完了。）

　　　"Honestly speaking, I have spent all my money."

2. 老实说，今天的菜真不好吃。

   （老實説，今天的菜真不好吃。）

   "Honestly speaking, the dishes today are really bad."

五. 判/判... *verb*: to sentence

   1. 判我有罪是不公平的。

      （判我有罪是不公平的。）

      "It is not fair to pronounce me guilty."

   2. 法官要判他十五年徒刑。

      （法官要判他十五年徒刑。）

      "The judge will sentence him to 15 years."

六. V + 到底/到底 V + *verbal complement*: to do something to the end

   1. 判我有罪是不公平的，我要上诉到底。

      （判我有罪是不公平的，我要上訴到底。）

      "It is not fair to pronounce me guilty. I will appeal all the way."

   2. 我不同意他的看法，我要跟他辩论到底。

      （我不同意他的看法，我要跟他辯論到底。）

      "I don't agree with him. I am going to debate with him to the end."

【补充辞汇/補充辭彙】

犯罪用语(word associated with crimes)：

大屠杀（殺）	dàtúshā	n.	massacre
从犯	cóngfàn	n.	accomplice
犯人	fànrén	n.	criminal
嫌犯	xiánfàn	n.	suspect
主谋（謀）	zhǔmóu	n.	conspirator

抢劫〔搶〕	qiǎngjié	v./n.	to rob; robbery
失职〔職〕	shīzhí	v.	to neglect one's duty
凶手〔兇〕	xiōngshǒu	n.	murderer
凶器〔兇〕	xiōngqì	n.	weapon
人质〔質〕	rénzhì	n.	hostage
妨害公务〔務〕	fánghàigōngwù	v.p.	to interfere with public functions
妨害自由	fánghàizìyóu	v.p.	to violate personal liberty
非法入境	fēifǎrùjìng	v.p.	to immigrate illegally
非法交易	fēifǎjiāoyì	n.p./v.p.	illegal transaction
非法堕胎	fēifǎduòtāi	n.p./v.p.	illegal abortion
拒捕	jùbǔ	v.	to refuse arrest
受贿〔賄〕	shòuhuì	v.	to receive a bribe
劫机〔機〕	jiéjī	v.	(air) hijacking
重婚罪	chónghūnzuì	n.p.	bigamy, polygamy
叛国〔國〕	pànguó	n.p.	to commit treason
逃税	táoshuì	v.p./n.	to avoid tax; avoidance of tax
恐吓〔嚇〕	kǒnghè	v./n.	to intimidate; intimidation
贪污〔貪〕	tānwū	v./n.	to embezzle; embezzlement
通奸	tōngjiān	v./n.	to commit adultery; adultery
强奸	qiángjiān	v./n.	to rape; rape
贩毒〔販〕	fàndú	v.p.	drug trafficking
勒索	lèsuǒ	v./n.	to extort; extortion
敲诈	qiāozhà	v./n.	to blackmail; blackmail
过失杀人〔過〕	guòshīshārén	v.p.	manslaughter
乱伦〔亂倫〕	luànlún	v.	to commit incest
暗杀〔殺〕	ànshā	v.	to assassinate
违法〔違〕	wéifǎ	v.	to break the law
伪造文书〔僞書〕	wěizàowénshū	v.p	to forge a document
诽谤〔誹謗〕	fěibàng	v./n.	to slander; slander
谋杀未遂〔謀殺〕	móushāwèisuí	v.p.	attempted murder
强奸未遂	qiángjiānwèisuí	v.p.	attempted rape
纵火〔縱〕	zònghuǒ	v.	to commit arson

【练习】

一. 完成句子：

　　1. 我万万没想到 _____。

　　2. 身为法官，他竟然 _____。

　　3. 我们学校的预算一再 _____。

　　4. 在我看来，劫机的人应该判 _____。

　　5. 假如_____，我会不顾一切地

　　　_____。

二. 填空：

　　　　虐待、资深、万万、界、前夕、达、竟、
　　　　伤透了脑筋、据我所知、在乎

　　他是位 _____ 的老师，在教育 _____ 服务 _____ 三十年，教出了不少学生。他 _____ 没想到在离开学校 _____，自己_____ 成了大家批评的对象。这件事让他 _____，也伤透了心。听说他被批评的原因是 _____ 学生。不过， _____，他之所以打学生、骂学生是因为他非常 _____ 他们的进步。

四. 翻译:

Because they neglected their duty, they lost their jobs three years ago. Soon they became addicted to drugs. They spent all their money on drugs and could not afford their living expenses. In order to get drugs they committed such crimes as stealing, prostitution, blackmail, and so on. The judge has sentenced them each to 15 years of imprisonment.

五. 作文: 你觉得怎样才能解决美国的毒品问题?

【練習】

一. 完成句子：

1. 我萬萬沒想到 _____。

2. 身為法官，他竟然 _____。

3. 我們學校的預算一再 _____。

4. 在我看來，劫機的人應該判 _____。

5. 假如_____，我會不顧一切地

_____。

二. 填空：

> 虐待、資深、萬萬、界、前夕、達、竟、
> 傷透了腦筋、據我所知、在乎

他是位 _____ 的老師，在教育 _____ 服務 _____ 三十年，教出了不少學生。他 _____ 沒想到在離開學校 _____ ，自己 _____ 成了大家批評的對象。這件事讓他 _____ ，也傷透了心。聽說他被批評的原因是 _____ 學生。不過， _____ ，他之所以打學生、罵學生是因為他非常 _____ 他們的進步。

四. 翻譯：

　　Because they neglected their duty, they lost their jobs three years ago. Soon they became addicted to drugs. They spent all their money on drugs and could not afford their living expenses. In order to get drugs they committed such crimes as stealing, prostitution, blackmail, and so on. The judge has sentenced them each to 15 years of imprisonment.

五. 作文：你覺得怎樣才能解決美國的毒品問題？

【衍生活动】

讨论与辩论

以下是一些犯罪的情况（所用名字纯属虚构），如果你是公正的法官，你会给这些罪犯什么样的刑罚？请在课堂上说明理由。

1. 王大年为了得到自由而劫机。
2. 李福生因酒醉开车撞死了人。
3. 陈爱美非法堕胎。
4. 刘平贩卖大麻。
5. 赵子华写文章批评政府，但不合事实。
6. 林怡非法进入美国并打工。
7. 孙家明在美国、中国各有一个太太。
8. 吴海被老板解雇之后，纵火烧了老板的汽车。
9. 钱木强奸了他的表妹。
10. 郑云因拒捕杀了警察。

【衍生活動】

討論與辯論

以下是一些犯罪的情況〔所用名字純屬虛構〕，如果你是公正的法官，你會給這些罪犯甚麼樣的刑罰？請在課堂上說明理由。

1. 王大年為了得到自由而劫機。
2. 李福生因酒醉開車撞死了人。
3. 陳愛美非法墮胎。
4. 劉平販賣大麻。
5. 趙子華寫文章批評政府，但不合事實。
6. 林怡非法進入美國並打工。
7. 孫家明在美國、中國各有一個太太。
8. 吳海被老闆解雇之後，縱火燒了老闆的汽車。
9. 錢木強奸了他的表妹。
10. 鄭雲因拒捕殺了警察。

【第九課】

愛情

【课文】

谈情说爱

　　最近，吴先生陷入爱情的深渊，痛苦得无法自拔。他翻阅圣经寻求答案，看到圣经的哥林多前书上说："爱是恒久忍耐，又有恩慈，爱是不忌妒，爱是不自夸，不张狂，不作害羞的事，不求自己的益处，不轻易发怒，不计较别人的恶，不喜欢不义，只喜欢真理，凡事包容，凡事相信，凡事忍耐，爱是永不止息的。"多么令人感动的句子！但毕竟是"知易行难"。

　　这天，吴先生决定去院庙请教法师，希望法师能指点一条明路，让自己早日脱离苦海。

法师：　你最近为情所困吧？

吴先生：你怎么知道？

法师：　恋爱和怀孕一样都是瞒不住的。

吴先生：我今天上山，希望您能告诉我爱情到底是什么？

法师：　"如人饮水，冷暖自知。""爱情"是无法用语言下定义
　　　　的，因为凡是能定义的东西都有限。"爱情"得用真实的
　　　　心去感受，很难用言语说明。

吴先生：那么，您认为爱情有什么意义？

法师：　爱情像盐。有了它，人才能尝出人间的美味，有了爱情就
　　　　有了幸福，因为爱情可以给人带来生命的活力，也可以让
　　　　人领悟生活的价值。爱情也是甜蜜的陷阱，目的是让人类

绵延不绝。人是大自然的一部分，很难逃出自然的规律。

吴先生：您认为人对爱情的态度会因年龄而改变吗？

法师：　是的，年轻人随心所欲，玩弄爱情；中年人食髓知味，追随爱情；老年人寂寞无聊，回忆爱情。

吴先生：您能不能说说什么是真正的爱情？

法师：　真正的爱情是两个人彼此无条件地投降。请注意"彼此"、"无条件"、"投降"这三项缺一不可。爱情是两个人的事，只有一方努力，爱情不会长久。爱情就要"无私地爱这个人"可不是因为他有什么。"投降"的意思是放下武器，切断所有的利害关系。

吴先生：师父，听说您年轻时就出家了，这辈子大概没被爱情困扰过吧？

法师：　为了抵抗世间的诱惑，我曾在心里立下一块"此路不通"的牌子。可是，爱情似乎含笑而过，说："什么地方我都能去"。在成佛之前，凡人终究是凡人。

讨论题：
1. 谈谈你对课文所讨论的问题的看法。
2. 你同意圣经里给"爱"下的定义吗？
3. 请你给"爱"下个定义。
4. 请你举例说明"爱"、"爱情"、"喜欢"有什么不同。
5. 错爱一个人之后如何平衡自己？
6. 人为什么在饱受失恋痛苦后还愿意再谈恋爱？
7. 说一个最令你感动的爱情故事。
8. 如果上帝给你一份完美的爱你希望是那一种？为什么？〔夫妻之爱，朋友之爱，骨肉之爱，手足之爱，上帝之爱…〕

【課文】

談情說愛

　　最近，吳先生陷入愛情的深淵，痛苦得無法自拔。他翻閱聖經尋求答案，看到聖經的哥林多前書上說：「愛是恆久忍耐，又有恩慈，愛是不嫉妒，愛是不自誇，不張狂，不作害羞的事，不求自己的益處，不輕易發怒，不計較別人的惡，不喜歡不義，只喜歡真理，凡事包容，凡事相信，凡事忍耐，愛是永不止息的。」多麼令人感動的句子！但畢竟是「知易行難」。

　　這天，吳先生決定去寺院請教法師，希望法師能指點一條明路，讓自己早日脫離苦海。

法師：　你最近為情所困吧？

吳先生：你怎麼知道？

法師：　戀愛和懷孕一樣都是瞞不住的。

吳先生：我今天上山，希望您能告訴我愛情到底是甚麼？

法師：　「如人飲水，冷暖自知。」「愛情」是無法用語言下定義的，因為凡是能定義的東西都有限。「愛情」得用真實的心去感受，很難用言語說明。

吳先生：那麼，您認為愛情有甚麼意義？

法師：　愛情像鹽。有了它，人才能嚐出人間的美味，有了愛情就有了幸福，因為愛情可以給人帶來生命的活力，也可以讓人領悟生活的價值。愛情也是甜蜜的陷穽，目的是讓人類綿延不絕。人是大自然的一部分，很難逃出自然的規律。

吳先生：您認爲人對愛情的態度會因年齡而改變嗎？

法師：　是的，年輕人隨心所欲，玩弄愛情；中年人食髓知味，追隨愛情；老年人寂寞無聊，回憶愛情。

吳先生：您能不能說說甚麼事真正的愛情？

法師：　真正的愛情是兩個人彼此無條件地投降。請注意"彼此"、"無條件"、"投降"這三項缺一不可。愛情是兩個人的事，只有一方努力，愛情不會長久。愛情就要"無私地愛這個人"可不是因爲他有甚麼。"投降"的意思是放下武器，切斷所有的利害關係。

吳先生：師父，聽說您年輕時就出家了，這輩子大概沒被愛情困擾過吧？

法師：　爲了抵抗世間的誘惑，我曾在心裏立下一塊"此路不通"的牌子。可是，愛情似乎含笑而過，說："甚麼地方我都能去"。在成佛之前，凡人終究是凡人。

討論題：

1. 談談你對課文所討論的問題的看法。
2. 你同意聖經裡給"愛"下的定義嗎？
3. 請你給"愛"下個定義。
4. 請你舉例說明"愛"、"愛情"、"喜歡"有甚麼不同。
5. 錯愛一個人之後如何平衡自己？
6. 人爲甚麼在飽受失戀痛苦後還願意再談戀愛？
7. 說一個最令你感動的愛情故事。
8. 如果上帝給你一份完美的愛你希望是那一種？爲甚麼？（夫妻之愛，朋友之愛，骨肉之愛，手足之愛，上帝之愛…）

【生词/生詞】

1. 陷入	xiànrù	v.	to fall into
2. 爱情（愛）	àiqíng	n.	love
3. 深渊（淵）	shēnyuān	n.	abyss
4. 痛苦	tòngkǔ	adj./n.	(to be) sad; suffering
5. 翻阅（閱）	fānyuè	v.	to browse, to read
6. 圣经（聖經）	shèngjīng	n.	Bible
7. 答案	dá'àn	n.	answer
8. 哥林多前书（書）	gēlínduōqiánshū	n.p.	1 Corinthians
9. 恒久	héngjiǔ	adj.	everlasting
10. 忍耐	rěnnài	v./n.	to restrain; restrain
11. 恩慈	ēncí	n.	kindness
12. 忌妒（嫉）	jìdù	v.	to be jealous
13. 自夸（誇）	zìkuā	v.	to praise oneself
14. 张狂（張）	zhāngkuáng	v.	to be insolent
15. 害羞	hàixiū	v.	to be shy, bashful
16. 益处（處）	yìchù	n.	benefit
17. 轻易（輕）	qīngyì	adv.	easily
18. 发怒（發）	fānù	v.	to become angry
19. 计较（計較）	jìjiào	v.	to fuss about
20. 恶（惡）	è	n./adj.	evil intention; (to be) evil
21. 真理	zhēnlǐ	n.	truth
22. 包容	bāoróng	v.	to forgive
23. 盼望	pànwàng	v.	to expect
24. 止息	zhǐxī	v.	to stop
25. 毕竟（畢）	bìjìng	adv.	after all
26. 知易行难（難）	zhīyìxíngnán	v.p.	to be easy to know and hard to do
27. 寺院	sìyuàn	n.	temple

28. 法师（師）	fǎshī	n.	(title) Buddhist priest
29. 脱离（脫離）	tuōlí	v.	to get away from
30. 怀孕（懷）	huáiyùn	v.	to be pregnant
31. 瞒不住（滿）	mánbúzhù	v.p.	cannot hide
32. 定义（義）	dìngyì	n.	definition
33. 领悟（領）	lǐngwù	v.	to understand
34. 价值（價）	jiàzhí	n.	significance, value
35. 甜蜜	tiánmì	adj.	(to be) sweet
36. 陷阱	xiànjǐng	n.	trap
37. 绵延不绝	miányánbùjué	v.p.	to be everlasting
38. 自然规律（规）	zìránguīlǜ	n.	natural law
39. 随心所欲（随）	suíxīnsuǒyù	v.p.	to do whatever one wants
40. 玩弄	wánnòng	v.	to play with
41. 食随知味（随）	shísuízhīwèi	v.p.	to experience and savor
42. 追随（随）	zhuīsuí	v.	to pursue
43. 寂寞无聊	jìmòwúliáo	v.p.	to be lonely and bored
44. 彼此	bǐcǐ	adv.	each other
45. 投降	tóuxiáng	v.	to surrender
46. 武器	wǔqì	n.	weapon
47. 切断（斷）	qiēduàn	v.	to break, to cut off
48. 最终（終）	zuìzhōng	adv.	finally
49. 困绕（繞）	kùnrǎo	v.	to be puzzled
50. 抵抗	dǐkàng	v.	to resist
51. 诱惑（誘）	yòuhuò	v./n.	to seduce; seduction
52. 立	lì	v.	to erect (a sign)
53. 此路不通（通）	cǐlùbùtōng	v.p.	dead end (of a street)
54. 牌子	páizi	n.	sign
55. 似乎	sìhū	v.	to seem as if
56. 含笑而过（過）	hánxiào'érguò	v.p.	to pass with a smile
57. 凡人	fánrén	n.	ordinary human being

【句型】

一. 凡是...都...; *conjunction...adv...*: whatever..., all

    1. 凡是爱情小说他都喜欢看。

      （凡是愛情小說他都喜歡看。）

      "He likes to read all novels about love and romance."

    2. 凡是去过中国的学生都参观过长城。

      （凡是去過中國的學生都參觀過長城。）

      "All those students who have been to China have visited the Great Wall."

二. 有了..., 就有了...; *verb phrase*: when one has ..., he/she will have... (The first clause introduces a condition). Simlilar patterns are: 有了......才能 Only when one has ... then he/she can ...

    1. 有了爱情, 就有了一切。

      （有了愛情, 就有了一切。）

      "When a person has love, he or she has everything."

    2. 有了爱情, 人才能尝出人间的美味。

      （有了愛情, 人才能嚐出人間的美味。）

      "Only when you have love can you taste the sweetness of life."

三. 犯...错误/犯...錯誤 *verb phrase*: to make ... a mistake

    1. 他经常犯语法错误。

      （他經常犯語法錯誤。）

      "He often makes grammar errors."

    2. 犯错误没关系, 只要能改正就是好学生。

      （犯錯誤沒關係, 只要能改正就是好學生。）

      "It is okay to make mistakes. As long as you correct your mistakes, you are a good student."

四. 最终/最終 *adverb*: eventually, in the end

1. 如果他们的爱情不是建立在相互信任的基础上，最终他们的关系一定
会破裂。

（如果他們的愛情不是建立在相互信任的基礎上，最終他們的關系一定
會破裂。）

"If their love is not based on mutual trust, their relationship will break
up in the end."

2. 最终她跟她的第一个男朋友结婚了。

（最終她跟她的第一個男朋友結婚了。）

"Finally, she married her first boyfriend."

五. 什么、哪里、谁...都（不）/甚麼、哪裏、誰...都（不）　+ verb ...; *Emphatic
structure*: whatever, wherever, whoever, etc.

1. 他谁都爱，甚至爱那些恨他的人。

（他誰都愛，甚至愛那些恨他的人。）

"He loves everyone, even those who hate him."

2. 他失恋了，现在对什么都毫无兴趣。

（他失戀了，現在對甚麼都毫無興趣。）

"He was very disappointed in love. Now he is not interested in anything."

3. 他哪儿都去，连冰岛那么冷的地方他也想去。

（他哪兒都去，連冰島那麼冷的地方他也想去。）

"He travels everywhere. He even wants to go to a place as cold as Iceland."

【语法/語法】

代词的语用功能/代詞的語用功能
(Discourse Function of Pronouns)

All students who use this book must have learned how to use different pronouns in Chinese; however, you might not know when pronouns have to be used in discourse or when they can be omitted. This section will give a brief description of the functions of prounouns in Chinese discourse. Generally speaking, pronouns in Chinese can be omitted if they are understood in a given context. For instance:

1. 我沒做晚饭，所以到现在还没吃饭呢！
   （我沒做晚飯，所以到現在還沒吃飯呢！）
   "I did not cook dinner, so (I) have not eaten yet.
2.   A: 吃了晚饭了吗？/吃了晚飯了嗎？
        "Have (you) had your dinner?"
      B: 还沒呢！/還沒呢！"
        "(I) have not eaten yet."

The topic/subject in 1 is "I", which is omitted in the second clause because it is clear from the context that the person who has not eaten yet is the one who did not cook the dinner. In (A) of the example 2, the second person pronoun is omitted, which most likely happens when two acquaintances meet and one asks the other the question in (A). In this case, "you" does not need to be specified because there is no other possible reference in that discourse. Similarly, to answer the question in (A), "I" does not need to be specified either.

Students whose native language is Indo-European might find it difficult to learn the function of Chinese pronouns since they can be omitted much more often than those in their native languages. There are two basic principles governing the use of Chinese pronouns: 1) pronouns must be specified by the speaker the first time they are used in discourse; 2) additionally, pronouns must be used when they cannot be understood by both the speaker and the listener in the given context. For instance, at the beginning of a conversation when a speaker establishes a topic, the topic pronoun cannot be omitted, but once the topic pronoun is established, it can be omitted as shown in 3.

3.　　Clause 1: 喂，老王，/喂，老王，
　　　　Clause 2: 今天有事吗？/今天有事嗎？
　　　　Clause 2: 没有的话，/沒有的話，
　　　　Clause 3: 我们去看电影好吗？/我們去看電影好嗎？
　　　　Clause 4: 然后还可以到公园转转。/然後還可以到公園轉轉。
　　　　Clause 5: 我在家里呆烦了，/我在家裡呆煩了，
　　　　Clause 6: 很想到外边去。/很想到外邊去。
　　　　Clause 7: 怎么样？/怎麼樣？
　　　　Clause 8: 去不去？/去不去？

"Hello, elder Wang, are (you) free today? If (you) do not have anything to do, we can go to see a movie. Then (we) can go to the park and take a walk. I am pretty bored at home, and (I) really want to go out. What do (you) think? Do (you) want to go (to see the movie and to the park) or not?"

Notice that the second person is omitted in the first two clauses. This is because both of them refer to Lao Wang, which is specified at the very beginning of the conversation. On the other hand, the first person pronoun "我们" in Clause 3 cannot be omitted because it is a new topic and is introduced for the first time in the discourse. In Clause 4, however, it is not new anymore, so it does not need to be specified. This is also true of Clauses 5-6. However, the situation of Clauses 7-8 is somewhat different from the rest of the clauses in the paragraph since the topic pronoun "you" is not mentioned in the immediately preceding clause, but is omitted. This is due to the setting of the conversation when the reference can be no one other than the listener (the second person pronoun).

【补充词汇／補充詞彙】

友情、婚姻 (Words associated with friendship and marriage):

交朋友	jiāo péngyǒu	v.p.	to make friends
抛弃 （棄）	pāoqì	v.	to desert
忘记 （記）	wàngjì	v.	to forget
酒肉	jiǔròu	n.	fair-weather
知心	zhīxīn	adj.	heart to heart
忠诚 （誠）	zhōngchéng	adj.	(to be) devoted
无私 （無）	wúsī	adj.	(to be) unselfish
牢固	láogù	adj.	(to be) firm
终生 （終）	zhōngshēng	adj./n.	(to be) life-long; whole life
坦率	tǎnshuài	adj.	(to be) frank
可靠	kěkào	adj.	(to be) dependable
亲密 （親）	qīnmì	adj.	(to be) intimate
纯洁 （純潔）	chúnjié	adj.	(to be) pure
友谊 （誼）	yǒuyí	n.	friendship
建立	jiànlì	v.	to establish
保持	bǎochí	v.	to maintain
关系 （關係）	guānxì	n.	relationship
增进 （進）	zēngjìn	v.	to enhance
珍视 （視）	zhēnshì	v.	to treasure
一见钟情 （見、鍾）	yíjiànzhōngqíng	v.p.	to fall in love with at first sight
向...求婚	xiàng...qiúhūn	v.p.	to propose marriage to ...
跟...订婚 （訂）	gēn...dìnghūn	v.p.	to become engaged to ...
跟...结婚 （結）	gēn...jiéhūn	v.p.	to marry
跟...离婚 （離）	gēn...líhūn	v.p.	to divorce
取消婚约 （約）	qǔxiāohūnyuē	v.p.	to cancel an engagement
婚礼 （禮）	hūnlǐ	n.	wedding

【练习】

一. 完成句子:

　　1. 凡是有钱的人 _____。

　　2. 有了爱情 _____。

　　3. 他什么都 _____。

　　4. 他上山去请教法师，目的是 _____。

二. 根据本课的语法解释去掉下列短文中多余的人称代词。

　　我很尊敬我的老师，他与人为善，与书为友。他也非常关心他的学生。他每天早起晚睡，日以继夜的工作。可是在我看来，他太注重自己的工作和研究。他不懂得生活的乐趣。他对孩子关心也不够。他的孩子们虽然爱他，但是他们有的时候对爸爸不太满意。他们觉得爸爸给他们的时间太少。

三. 用中文解释下列词语:

1. 知易行难

2. 随心所欲

3. 食髓知味

4. 此路不通

四. 造句： In order to demonstrate your understanding of the following phrases, you need to write short paragraphs instead of single sentences.

1. 最终

2. 毕竟

3. 彼此

4. 有了......才

五. 作文：在你看来什么样的爱最重要？ (Your essay should consist of your opinion and some supporting details.)

【練習】

一. 完成句子:

    1. 凡是有錢的人 _____。

    2. 有了愛情 _____。

    3. 他甚麼都 _____。

    4. 他上山去請教法師，目的是 _____。

二. 根據本課的語法解釋去掉下列短文中多餘的人稱代詞。

    我很尊敬我的老師，他與人為善，與書為友。他也非常關心他的學生。他每天早起晚睡，日以繼夜的工作。可是在我看來，他太注重自己的工作和研究。他不懂得生活的樂趣。他對孩子關心也不夠。他的孩子們雖然愛他，但是他們有的時候對爸爸不太滿意。他們覺得爸爸給他們的時間太少。

三. 用中文解釋下列詞語:

1. 知易行難

2. 隨心所欲

3. 食髓知味

4. 此路不通

四. 造句: In order to demonstrate your understanding of the following phrases, you need to write short paragraphs instead of single sentences.

1. 最終

2. 畢竟

3. 彼此

4. 有了......才

五. 作文: 在你看來甚麼樣的愛最重要? (Your essay should consist of your opinion and some supporting details.)

【衍生活动】

标点与翻译

请将以下短文标上标点，翻译成你的母语，并指出哪一句的人称代词省略了（参考标点符号： ，。、？：「」）：

顾先生的交友哲学

顾先生三十五岁了还没结婚他的朋友都替他著急但是顾先生只愿意慢慢地等他有一套选太太的哲学而这套哲学来自巴哈（BACH）的音乐这是什么意思呢顾先生认为选太太和交女朋友大不相同女朋友可以像流行音乐而太太就得像巴哈音乐流行的音乐往往有时间性在短期内能让人著迷(to make someone fall in love)等流行一过就没人再愿意听它了巴哈的音乐不容易让人著迷但是只要你爱上它一辈子就少不了它并且百听不厌最后它就成了你生命的一部份换一句话说找太太就是要找一个跟你一起让生命成长的人以前顾先生也交过许多女朋友但是都没结成婚也许他的眼光太高了如果你是顾先生的朋友请替他找一位合适的小姐

【衍生活動】

標點與翻譯

請將以下短文標上標點，翻譯成你的母語，並指出哪一句的人稱代詞省略了
（參考標點符號： ， 。 、 ？ ： 「」 ）。

顧先生的交友哲學

顧先生三十五歲了還沒結婚他的朋友都替他著急但是顧先生只願意慢慢地等他有一套選太太的哲學而這套哲學來自巴哈（BACH）的音樂這是甚麼意思呢顧先生認為選太太和交女朋友大不相同女朋友可以像流行音樂而太太就得像巴哈音樂流行的音樂往往有時間性在短期內能讓人著迷(to make someone fall in love)等流行一過就沒人再願意聽它了巴哈的音樂不容易讓人著迷但是只要你愛上它一輩子就少不了它並且百聽不厭最後它就成了你生命的一部份換一句話說找太太就是要找一個跟你一起讓生命成長的人以前顧先生也交過許多女朋友但是都沒結成婚也許他的眼光太高了如果你是顧先生的朋友請替他找一位合適的小姐

【第十課】

貧民

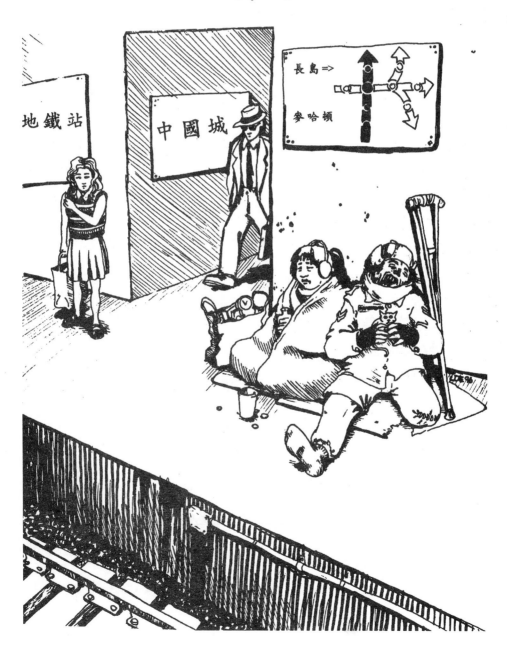

【课文】

流浪汉的对话

老王： 喂，来块儿披萨饼吧！

老李： 谢谢，你自个儿慢用，但愿我现在有一口酒喝。

老王： 想开点儿，"借酒浇愁愁更愁"有谁愿意沦落到无家可归的地步呢？还不都是命！你看住在这个地铁车站的人，谁没有一段伤心的往事呢？埋怨、悲伤、愤怒都解决不了问题，想办法让自己愉快一点吧！

老李： 我真不甘心，这世界对我们太不公平了。从小我就是一个努力上进的人，虽然家庭并不富裕没有给我太多经济上的帮助，但是我仍然靠着贷款念完了研究院。在漫长的求学过程中我吃足了苦，放弃了年轻人能享受的快乐，甚至把交女朋友的时间都省下来念书做实验，过着近乎清教徒的生活。我以为苦几年就会熬出头的，没想到一次工作上的失败就把我搞得倾家荡产，最后为了付律师费连房子也卖了，更不幸的是我染上了酗酒的毛病。我现在盼望的只是"一醉解千愁"。

老王： 跟你比起来我简直是魔鬼了。十七岁那年我在老家，听从父母之命，结了婚。那是一个没有爱情基础的婚姻，我打定主意要早日脱离苦海。于是，等媳妇生了儿子，我也尽了传宗接代的责任后，就离家出走，偷渡到美国来了。旧金山是我到美国的第一站，当时我既没有一技之长也没有身份，只能在餐馆打零工。为了一张绿卡，我日以继夜地工作，十年后终于爬上了大厨的位置，也娶了老板的女儿，本来以为从此可以高枕无忧等着作老板，谁知道一把火把餐厅烧得片瓦不留，不久老婆也带着所有的积蓄跟别人走了。我相信，这是老天在惩罚我，是报应啊！

老李： 现在你想不想回家看看老婆，看看孩子呢？

老王： 我有什么脸回去呢？年轻的时候没有善尽为人夫、为人父的责任，临老又不能衣锦还乡，即使我能弄到一张机票，我也不敢回去，真的是"有家不能归"。倒是你，年纪还轻又有专业知识、技能，趁早把酒戒了，一切都可以从头来。地铁站毕竟不是能久待的地方，听说市政府要派人赶我们离开这里。我打算过几天去找个零活做，混口饭吃，免得冬天来了冻死在街头。

老李： 重新开始，我也试过，不过谈何容易！酒是穿肠毒药，我何尝不知道？只是当失败的阴影压得我透不过气来的时候，酒就成了救命的好东西。

老王： 以我这个旁观者看来，你的问题并没有那么严重，谁在工作的时候不犯一点儿错？你就是被自己要求完美的个性给害了。振作一点吧！

老李： 谢谢，没想到在这样狼狈的情况下还能碰到您这种热心人，可惜我的信用卡被停用了，否则我一定请您好好的喝一杯。

【課文】

流浪漢的對話

老王： 喂，來塊兒披薩餅吧！

老李： 謝謝，你自個兒慢用，但願我現在有一口酒喝。

老王： 想開點兒，"借酒澆愁愁更愁"有誰願意淪落到無家可歸的地步呢？還不都是命！你看住在這個地鐵車站的人，誰沒有一段傷心的往事呢？埋怨、悲傷、憤怒都解決不了問題，想辦法讓自己愉快一點吧！

老李： 我真不甘心，這世界對我們太不公平了。從小我就是一個努力上進的人，雖然家庭並不富裕沒有給我太多經濟上的幫助，但是我仍然靠着貸款唸完了研究院。在漫長的求學過程中我吃足了苦，放棄了年輕人能享受的快樂，甚至把交女朋友的時間都省下來唸書做實驗，過着近乎清教徒的生活。我以為苦幾年就會熬出頭的，沒想到一次工作上的失敗就把我搞得傾家蕩產，最後為了付律師費連房子也賣了，更不幸的是我染上了酗酒的毛病。我現在盼望的只是"一醉解千愁"。

老王： 跟你比起來我簡直是魔鬼了。十七歲那年我在老家，聽從父母之命，結了婚。那是一個沒有愛情基礎的婚姻，我打定主意要早日脫離苦海。於是，等媳婦生了兒子，我也盡了傳宗接代的責任後，就離家出走，偷渡到美國來了。舊金山是我到美國的第一站，當時我既沒有一技之長也沒有身份，只能在餐館打零工。為了一張綠卡，我日以繼夜地工作，十年後終於爬上了大廚的位置，也娶了老板的女兒，本來以為從此可以高枕無憂等着作老板，誰知道一把火把餐廳燒得片瓦不留，不久老婆也帶着所有的積蓄跟別人走了。我相信，這是老天在懲罰我，是報應啊！

老李：　現在你想不想回家看看老婆，看看孩子呢？

老王：　我有甚麼臉回去呢？年輕的時候沒有善盡為人夫，為人父的責任，臨老又不能衣錦還鄉，即使我能弄到一張機票，我也不敢回去，真的是“有家不能歸”。倒是你，年紀還輕又有專業知識、技能，趁早把酒戒了，一切都可以從頭來。地鐵站畢竟不是能久待的地方，聽說市政府要派人趕我們離開這裏。我打算過幾天去找個零活做，混口飯吃，免得冬天來了凍死在街頭。

老李：　重新開始，我也試過，不過談何容易！酒是穿腸毒藥，我何嘗不知道？只是當失敗的陰影壓得我透不過氣來的時候，酒就成了救命的好東西。

老王：　以我這個旁觀者看來，你的問題並沒有那麼嚴重，誰在工作的時候不犯一點兒錯？你就是被自己要求完美的個性給害了。振作一點吧！

老李：　謝謝，沒想到在這樣狼狽的情況下還能碰到您這種熱心人，可惜我的信用卡被停用了，否則我一定請您好好的喝一杯。

讨论题:

1. 谈谈你对流浪汉的印象。
2. 为什么很多流浪汉酗酒?
3. 一个流浪汉在街头要钱,你给不给?为什么?
4. 非法移民过多对美国的经济会造成什么影响?
5. 你认为美国的社会福利政策还有哪些缺点?
6. 你有哪些方法可以让自己在年老的时候免于贫穷?
7. 如果你是一个市长或州长你会用什么方法消灭贫穷?

討論題:

1. 談談你對流浪漢的印象。
2. 為甚麼很多流浪漢酗酒?
3. 一個流浪漢在街頭要錢,你給不給?為甚麼?
4. 非法移民過多對美國的經濟會造成甚麼影響?
5. 你認為美國的社會福利政策還有哪些缺點?
6. 你有哪些方法可以讓自己在年老的時候免於貧窮?
7. 如果你是一個市長或州長你會用甚麼方法消滅貧窮?

【生词/生詞】

1. 流浪汉（漢）	liúlànghàn	n.	homeless man
2. 浇（澆）	jiāo	v.	to pour liquid on
3. 沦落（淪）	lúnluò	v.	to fall low
4. 无家可归（無歸）	wújiākěguī	adj. p.	(to be) homeless
5. 地步	dìbù	n.	situation
6. 命	mìng	n.	fate, order, command
7. 地铁（鐵）	dìxiàtiě	n.	subway
8. 车站（車）	chēzhàn	n.	(bus)stop, (train)terminal
9. 埋怨	mányuàn	n./v.	blame; to blame
10. 悲伤（傷）	bēishāng	n./v.	grief; to be grieved
11. 愤怒（憤）	fènnù	n./v.	indignation; to be angry
12. 甘心	gānxīn	v.	to be willing
13. 上进（進）	shàngjìn	adj.	making progress
14. 富裕	fùyù	adj.	(to be) wealthy
15. 仍然	réngrán	adv.	still
16. 贷款（貸）	dàikuǎn	n.	loan
17. 研究院	yánjiūyuàn	n.	graduate school
18. 漫长（長）	màncháng	adj.	long, endless
19. 放弃（棄）	fàngqì	v.	to abandon
20. 甚至	shènzhì	adv.	even
21. 近乎	jìnhū	adv.	almost
22. 熬出头（頭）	áochūtóu	v.p.	to bring an end to
23. 清教徒	qīngjiàotú	n.	Puritan
24. 失败（敗）	shībài	n./v.	failure; to be defeated
25. 倾家荡产（傾蕩產）	qīngjiādàngchǎn	adj.p.	to lose everything
26. 酗酒	xùjiǔ	v.p.	to drink excessively
27. 简直（簡）	jiǎnzhí	adv.	simply, extremely
28. 魔鬼	móguǐ	n.	devil

29. 听从 (聽從)	tīngcóng	v.	to obey
30. 基础 (礎)	jīchǔ	n.	basis, foundation
31. 传宗接代 (傳)	chuánzōngjiēdài	v.p.	to pass on to future generations
32. 偷渡	tōudù	v.	to secretly cross (e.g. seas)
33. 零工	línggōng	n.	part-time job
34. 日以继夜 (繼)	rìyǐjìyè	adv.p.	day and night
35. 终于 (終於)	zhōngyú	adv.	finally, in the end
36. 大厨	dàchú	n.	chief chef
37. 位置	wèizhì	n.	position
38. 娶	qǔ	v.	to marry (a woman)
39. 本来 (來)	běnlái	adv.	originally
40. 高枕无忧 (無憂)	gāozhěnwúyōu	v.p.	to be worry-free
41. 片瓦	piànwǎ	n.	a piece of tile
42. 积蓄 (積)	jīxù	n./v.	savings; to save (money)
43. 惩罚 (懲罰)	chéngfá	v.	to punish
44. 报应 (報應)	bàoyìng	n.	retribution
45. 临 (臨)	lín	adv.	right before
46. 衣锦还乡 (錦還鄉)	yījǐnhuánxiāng	v.p.	to return home in glory
47. 技能	jìnéng	n.	skill
48. 趁早	chènzǎo	adv.	before it is too late
49. 戒	jiè	v.	to give up (e.g. drinking)
50. 毒药 (藥)	dúyào	n.	poison
51. 阴影 (陰)	yīnyǐng	n.	shadow
52. 完美	wánměi	adj.	(to be) perfect
53. 振作	zhènzuò	v.	to cheer up
54. 狼狈 (狽)	lángbèi	adj.	(to be) awkward
55. 碰到	pèngdào	v.	to meet, to bump into
56. 热心 (熱)	rèxīn	adj.	(to be) warmhearted
57. 可惜	kěxī	v.	to pity
58. 否则 (則)	fǒuzé	adv.	otherwise
59. 福利	fúlì	n.	benefit

【句型】

一. 但愿/但願 *conjuctional phrase*: if only ..., I wish... This phrase introduces a sentence expressing speakers' wish.

1. 但愿我现在有一口酒喝。

（但願我現在有一口酒喝。）

"I wish I had some alcohol to drink now."

2. 但愿新上任的总统会解决贫穷的问题。

（但願新上任的總統會解決貧窮的問題。）

"I wish the newly elected president would solve the poverty problem."

二. 靠 +NP (+ VP); *verb*: rely on ...

1. 他靠着贷款念完了研究院。

（他靠着貸款唸完了研究院。）

"He relied on financial loans to finish graduate school."

2. 很多人靠爸爸妈妈的关系找到一个好工作，他们这样作公平吗？

（很多人靠爸爸媽媽的關係找到一個好工作，他們這樣作公平嗎？）

"Many people rely on their parents' connections to find a good job. Do you think this is fair?"

三. 在...过程中/在...過程中 *prepositional phrase*: during the time of ...

1. 在求学过程中，他为了交学费日以继夜地工作。

（在求學過程中，他爲了交學費日以繼夜地工作。）

"While he was attending school, he worked day and night to pay for his tuition."

2. 在竞选市长过程中，他犯了很多错误。

（在競選市長過程中，他犯了很多錯誤。）

"When he was running for mayor, he made many mistakes."

四. 跟...比起来/跟...比起來 *verb phrase*: compared with ...

1. 跟你比起来我真是太不幸了。

（跟你比起來我真是太不幸了。）

"Compared with you, I am very unlucky."

2. 跟日本比起来美国的汽车工业还有很长的路要走。

（跟日本比起來美國的汽車工業還有很長的路要走。）

"In comparison with Japan, the automobile industry in the United Sates has a long way to go."

五. 即使...也.../即使...也... ; *conjunction*: even though/if ...

1. 即使我能弄到一张机票也没脸回去见我的家人。

（即使我能弄到一張機票也沒臉回去見我的家人。）

"Even if I am able to get an airline ticket, I would still feel ashamed to go and visit my family."

2. 即使家庭富裕的孩子也不應該完全靠父母。

（即使我能弄到一張機票也沒臉回去見我的家人。）

"Even wealthy children should not depend entirely on their parents."

六. 毕竟/畢竟 *adverb*: after all

1. 地铁站毕竟不是能久呆的地方。

（地鐵站畢竟不是能久呆的地方。）

"After all, the subway is not a place where you could stay forever."

2. 你不要对他要求太高，他毕竟是个孩子。

（你不要對他要求太高，他畢竟是個孩子。）

"You should not expect too much of him. After all, he is just a kid."

七. 免得/免得 *verb phrase*: so as not to; so as to avoid ...

1. 他应该找个工作，混口饭吃，免得冬天来了冻死在街头。

（他應該找個工作，混口飯吃，免得冬天來了凍死在街頭。）

"He should find a job to feed himself so he can avoid being frozen to death on the street when winter comes."

2. 别让那个捣蛋鬼去你家，免得把你家弄得乱七八糟。

（別讓那個搗蛋鬼去你家，免得把你家弄得亂七八糟。）

"To avoid having him make a mess of your house, don't let that trouble-maker visit your home!"

八. 何尝/何嘗 *exclamatory phrase*: how could ... (One of the functions of this phrase is to be put before a negation word to form a rhetorical question. It is often used in the written style or formal style of speaking.)

1. 喝酒并不能解愁，我何尝不知道？只是酒瘾上来我没法控制自己。
   （喝酒並不能解愁，我何嘗不知道？只是酒癮上來我沒法控制自己。）

   "How could I not know that drinking cannot eliminate worries?

   When I cannot control myself, I am addicted to alcohol."

2. 那些流浪汉何尝不想过好日子？只是他们的命太不好了。
   （那些流浪漢何嘗不想過好日子？只是他們的命太不好了。）

   "How could those homeless people not want to live a good life? It is only that their fate is not very good."

九. 可惜/可惜 *verb phrase*: It is a pity (that ...).

1. 可惜我的信用卡被停用了，否则我可以请您去酒吧喝两杯。
   （可惜我的信用卡被停用了，否則我可以請您去酒吧喝兩盃。）

   "It is a pity that my credit card has expired; otherwise, I could take you to the bar to have a drink."

2. 他染上了吸毒的毛病，结果妻离子散，真可惜！
   （他染上了吸毒的毛病，結果妻離子散，真可惜！）

   "He became addicted to drugs. As a result, both his wife and his children left him. What a pity!

【语法/語法】

"使" 动词, "使" 動詞
(Causative Verbs)

Different languages have different ways of expressing causative actions: some languages use a suffix, while others use an independent morpheme/word/character. Mandarin belongs to the second category. There are several characters that convey the causative meaning in Mandarin. The most commonly used ones are 使, 让/讓, and 叫, and they are used in the structure of: NP1-causatve verb-NP2-verb, as shown below:

1. 这本书使（让）我真正了解到中国人的生活。

   （這本書使（讓）我真正瞭解到中國人的生活。）

   "This book made me fully understand the life of the Chinese people."

2. 老师让（叫）我们作一篇有关美国社会的作文。

   （老師讓（叫）我們作一篇有關美國社會的作文。）

   "The teacher asked us to write a paper about American society."

3. 你这么做叫（让/使）我很不好意思。

   （你這麼做叫（讓/使）我很不好意思。）

   "What you did embarrassed me greatly."

An immediate question that students may have is whether there is any difference among the three causative verbs, and if there is, how to distinguish them. The answer to the question is affirmative. The following is a brief description of the functions of the three causative verbs.

All three verbs can be translated into English as "make" (as shown in 3); however, they differ from one another in terms of 1) how the causative action proceeds them, 2) who causes the action, and 3) what meaning the causative verb has. According to our study, 使 is most likely to be used if the causative action is durative (to last for a period of time) and the causer is non-human (as shown in 1), otherwise 让/讓 or 叫 is used. Another difference between 使 and the other two is that 使 cannot express the meaning of "ask", whereas 让 and 叫 can. To differentiate 让 from 叫, on the other hand, one has to consider other functions of the two words. For instance, 让 can express the meaning of "allow", but 叫 cannot (as shown in 4). Furthermore, 叫 shows that the causer is willing to cause an action, whereas 让 does not express that willingness, at least not as strongly as 叫 (as illustrated in 5).

    4. 我父亲让我跟王先生结婚。/我父親讓我跟王先生結婚。

      "My father allowed me to marry Mr. Wang."

    5. 我父亲叫我跟王先生结婚。/我父親叫我跟王先生結婚。

      "My father let me (willingly) marry Mr. Wang."

With this brief description, students should have a general understanding of the function of the three causative verbs.

【补充词汇/補充詞彙】

贫困、灾难 (words associated with poverty and disaster):

乞丐	qǐgài	n.	begger
乞讨 （討）	qǐtǎo	v.	to beg
天灾 （災）	tiānzāi	n.	natural disaster
人祸 （禍）	rénhuò	n.	man-made disaster
失业 （業）	shīyè	v.p.	to lose one's job
地震	dìzhèn	n.	earthquake
旱灾 （災）	hànzāi	n.	drought (disaster)
涝灾 （澇災）	làozāi	n.	flood
灾区 （災區）	zāiqū	n.	disaster area
灾民 （災）	zāimín	n.	victims of a disaster
灾难 （災難）	zāinàn	n.	disaster, calamity
环境污染 （環）	huánjìngwūrǎn	n.p.	environmental pollution
贫困 （貧）	pínkùn	n.	poverty
贫困户 （貧）	pínkùnhù	n.p.	families in poverty
幸灾乐祸 （災樂禍）	xìngzāilèhuò	v.p.	to take pleasure in other people's misfortune

穷光蛋（窮）	qióngguāngdàn	n.p.	poor wretch
孤独（獨）	gūdú	adj.	(to be) lonely
孤儿	gū'ér	n.	orphan
保险（險）	bǎoxiǎn	v./n.	to insure; insurance
难民（難）	nànmín	n.	refugee
难兄难弟（難）	nànxiōngnàndì	n.p.	fellow sufferers
痛苦	tòngkǔ	n.	suffering
忍受	rěnshòu	v.	to bear (suffering)
减轻（減輕）	jiǎnqīng	v.	to reduce (suffering)
难以忍受（難）	nányǐrěnshòu	v.p.	to be difficult to bear
难以置信（難）	nányǐzhìxìn	v.p.	to be difficult to believe
难以想像（難）	nányǐxiǎngxiàng	v.p.	to be difficult to imagine

【练习】

一. 完成句子：

1. 依我看来，中国现在应该想办法控制人口的增长免得 ＿＿＿＿＿＿＿＿＿＿

＿＿＿＿＿＿＿＿＿＿＿＿＿＿。

2. 即使让我倾家荡产 ＿＿＿＿＿＿＿＿＿＿＿＿＿＿＿＿＿＿＿＿＿＿。

3. 可惜我 ＿＿＿＿＿＿＿＿ 否则 ＿＿＿＿＿＿＿＿＿＿＿＿＿＿＿＿。

4. 在谈恋爱的过程中，＿＿＿＿＿＿＿＿＿＿＿＿＿＿＿＿＿＿＿＿＿。

5. 还有 ＿＿＿＿＿＿ 我就要毕业了，但愿 ＿＿＿＿＿＿＿＿＿＿＿＿＿。

二. 选词填空：

> 免得、终于、贷款、没想到、人们说、虽然、靠、
> 在...过程中、被

　　从小他就是一个努力上进的人，虽然父母经济条件很好，但是他不＿＿＿＿＿父母，而是靠 ＿＿＿＿＿＿ 和周末打工念完了研究院。＿＿＿＿＿＿漫长的求学 ＿＿＿＿＿＿ 他吃够了苦，放弃了年轻人能享受的快乐。他的运气还算不错。毕业以后经过努力 ＿＿＿＿＿＿ 在一家大公司找到了一份好工作，进入了白领阶层(stratum)。但是 ＿＿＿＿＿＿ 由于美国经济不景气，他 ＿＿＿＿＿＿ 公司解雇了。最近他自己开了一家健身中心，这样他可以赚些钱 ＿＿＿＿＿＿ 以后过流浪汉的日子。他 ＿＿＿＿＿＿ 工作辛苦，每天早起晚睡，但是至少不必受别人的摆布，自己爱作什么就作什么。＿＿＿＿＿＿ 在美国越来越多的人喜欢自己开店当老板。你呢？你以后打算作什么？

三. 用中文解释下列词语：

1. 衣锦还乡

2. 一醉解千愁

3. 高枕无忧

四. 造句：(In order to demonstrate your understanding of the following phrases, you need to write short paragraphs instead of single sentences.)

1. 跟...比起来 (for comparison structures)

2. 何尝 (for rhetorical questions)

3. 连 ... 都 ..., 更不幸的是... (for enumeration structures)

4. 等... 就 ... 然后 ... (for time-order structures)

5. 让... 使... 叫... (for causative structures)

五. 作文：在美国为什么有很多无家可归的人？你认为怎么样才能解决贫民的问题？(You may find the following necessary for your composition: 1. For cause-effect structures: 之所以... 是因为; 2) for listing structures: 首先... 第二... 第三...; ... 的主要原因是... 再加上...)

【練習】

一. 完成句子：

1. 依我看來，中國現在應該想辦法控制人口的增長免得 _____

　　_____。

2. 即使讓我傾家蕩產 _____。

3. 可惜我 _____ 否則 _____。

4. 在談戀愛的過程中，_____。

5. 還有 _____ 我就要畢業了，但願 _____。

二. 選詞填空：

　　免得、終於、助學貸款、沒想到、人們說、雖然、靠、
　　在...過程中、被

　　從小他就是一個努力上進的人，雖然父母經濟條件很好，但是他不 _____父母，而是靠自己的 _____ 和週末打工唸完了研究院。_____ 漫長的求學 _____ 他吃夠了苦，放棄了年輕人能享受的快樂。他的運氣還算不錯。畢業以後經過努力 _____ 在一家大公司找到了一份好工作，進入了白領階層(stratum)。但是 _____ 由於美國經濟不景氣，他 _____ 公司解雇了。最近他自己開了一家健身中心，這樣他可以賺些錢 _____ 以後過流浪漢的日子。他 _____ 工作辛苦，每天早起晚睡，但是至少不必受別人的擺布，自己愛作甚麼就作甚麼。_____ 在美國越來越多的人喜歡自己開店當老板。你呢？你以後打算作甚麼？

三. 用中文解釋下列詞語：

1. 衣錦還鄉

2. 一醉解千愁

3. 高枕無憂

四. 造句：(In order to demonstrate your understanding of the following phrases, you need to write short paragraphs instead of single sentences.)

1. 跟...比起來 (for comparison structures)

2. 何嘗 (for rhetorical questions)

3. 連 ... 都 ...，更不幸的是... (for enumeration structures)

4. 等... 就 ... 然後 ... (for time-order structures)

5. 讓... 使... 叫... (for causative structures)

五. 作文：在美國為甚麼有很多無家可歸的人？你認為怎麼才能解決貧民的問題？ (You may find the following necessary for your composition: 1. For cause-effect structures 之所以... 是因為; 2) for listing structures: 首先... 第二... 第三...; ... 的主要原因是... 再加上...)

【衍生活动】

讨论问题：如何帮助贫民？

　　美国政府现在有一项计划，是让大都市的贫穷家庭搬到生活条件较佳、工作机会较多的地区居住，搬家费及那个家庭找到工作前的生活费都由政府负担。对于这项计划，你赞成还是反对？为什么？请在课堂上和老师同学讨论。请参考下面的理由。

反对的理由：
1. 完全反对，没有理由。16%
2. 这个计划不实际。9%
3. 受帮助的家庭会产生新贫民区。7%
4. 对政府、人民来说花费太大。7%
5. 对政府的压力太大。6%
6. 更简单的是把机会带入贫民区。6%
7. 想法太乐观。6%
8. 受帮助的人对工作没兴趣。4%
9. 钱应该是赚来的不是别人给的。3%
10. 政府没有权力管这件事。2%

赞成的理由：
1. 赞成，没有理由。10%
2. 贫穷家庭同意这项计划，就赞成。6%
3. 有适当的政策，就赞成。6%
4. 这是得到更美好生活的机会。5%

<u>赞成的理由</u> 〔继续〕：

    5. 这种工作确实合乎道德。4%

    6. 可以试试看。4%

    7. 可以得到人力。 2%

    8. 不管贫民，以后的负担会更重。1%

    9. 人类应该彼此帮助。8%

  10. 不管贫民问题，会让国家丢脸。1%

<u>讨论题</u>：

    1. 你赞不赞成此项计划，为什么？

    2. 请根据上表分析一下现代美国人对贫穷的看法。

    3. 为什么美国贫民的问题一天比一天严重？

    4. 用所缴的税帮助同胞是国民的责任吗？

【衍生活動】

討論問題：如何幫助貧民？

　　美國政府現在有一項計划，是讓大都市的貧窮家庭搬到生活條件較佳、工作機會較多的地區居住，搬家費及那個家庭找到工作前的生活費都由政府負擔。對於這項計划，你贊成還是反對？爲甚麼？請在課堂上和老師同學討論。請參考下面的理由。

反對的理由：
1. 完全反對，沒有理由。16%
2. 這個計劃不實際。9%
3. 受幫助的家庭會產生新貧民區。7%
4. 對政府、人民來說花費太大。7%
5. 對政府的壓力太大。6%
6. 更簡單的是把機會帶入貧民區。6%
7. 想法太樂觀。6%
8. 受幫助的人對工作沒興趣。4%
9. 錢應該是賺來的不是別人給的。3%
10. 政府沒有權力管這件事。2%

贊成的理由：
1. 贊成，沒有理由。10%
2. 貧窮家庭同意這項計劃，就贊成。6%
3. 有適當的政策，就贊成。6%
4. 這是得到更美好生活的機會。5%

贊成的理由 〔繼續〕：

    5. 這種工作確實合乎道德。4%

    6. 可以試試看。4%

    7. 可以得到人力。 2%

    8. 不管貧民，以後的負擔會更重。1%

    9. 人類應該彼此幫助。8%

   10. 不管貧民問題，會讓國家丟臉。1%

討論題：

    1. 你贊不贊成此項計划，為甚麼？

    2. 請根據上表分析一下現代美國人對貧窮的看法。

    3. 為甚麼美國貧民的問題一天比一天嚴重？

    4. 用所繳的稅幫助同胞是國民的責任嗎？

中國文化

〔课文〕

教授与学生谈文化问题

教授： 时间过得真快，一转眼你进博士班已经三年了，论文题目定了没有？

学生： 这正是几个月来我最苦恼的问题，对我来说，花两、三年的时间，写出一本论文换个文凭并不是什么了不起的事。只是，我不希望浪费自己的生命去制造一些文字垃圾，写出于人于己都毫无用处的东西。老师，您一辈子研究儒家思想，依您看我应该和您一样，一辈子走这条路吗？

教授： 这真的是一个很难回答的问题。你觉得花一辈子去研究中国的儒家思想不值得？那么，你三年前的理想到哪去了？

学生： 我以为儒家思想在先秦就已经完成了它的历史责任，与其花时间去弄那些旧东西，倒不如想办法开创这个时代的新思想。

教授： 你跟著我研究了好多年，你还记得我说过的一个比喻吗？在一条街上，有米店、水果行、菜市场、药房等等和民生息息相关的小店。店里面也卖各种民生必需品。对中国人而言，儒家就好像是开米店的，道家、佛教和西方思想则是卖菜、卖水果的。没有药、没有菜、没有水果，我们还能活下去；没有米，我们就会饿死。当然，人光吃米不够，会营养不良，所以在历史上也能找到中国采用其他思想治国的例子。你所谓的新思想必须建立在传统的根基上，而儒家思想就是中国文化的根，根毁了，枝叶也就凋零了。

学生： 我记得您说的例子，不过，换个角度来看，少吃米或是偶尔改吃面包也不错。

教授： 我没有理由否定你的说法。我更不是一个食古不化的人，然而，中国走向西方，已经是无人能挡的时代潮流了。除非你真的对西学有兴趣，要不然大可不必跟著潮流跑。看看现在的社会风气，青少年唱英文歌、吃汉堡包；大学生念外文教科书、读翻译小说；就连专家学者发表意见的时候，也要带上两句洋文，来证明自己的深度。这样下去，用不了五十年中国人的意识形态就会跟西方人完全一样。

学生： 我会再想想您的话。不过我也相信，每个时代的人都得被迫放弃一些传统，要是我只在一些不实际的东西上下工夫，那不过就是浪费时间而已！对现在、对未来的中国人都没有好处。

教授： 「人各有志」，我不能勉强你，你也不是第一个跟我讨论这种问题的学生。无论未来的研究方向是什么，我都希望你做个有良知的知识分子。

学生： 老师，也许有一天我会辜负您的期望，但是我绝不会忘记您的教诲。

〔課文〕

教授與學生談文化問題

教授： 時間過得真快，一轉眼你進博士班已經三年了，論文題
目定了沒有？

學生： 這正是幾個月來我最苦惱的問題，對我來說，花兩、三
年的時間，寫出一本論文換個文憑並不是甚麼了不起的
事。只是，我不希望浪費自己的生命去製造一些文字垃
圾，寫出於人、於己都毫無用處的東西。老師，您一輩
子研究儒家思想，依您看，我應該和您一樣，一輩子走
這條路嗎？

教授： 這真的是一個很難回答的問題。你覺得花一輩子去研究
中國的儒家思想不值得？那麼，你三年前的理想到哪去
了？

學生： 我以為儒家思想在先秦就已經完成了它的歷史責任，與
其花時間去弄那些舊東西，倒不如想辦法開創這個時代
的新思想。

教授： 你跟著我研究了好多年，你還記得我說過的一個比喻嗎？
在一條街上，有米店、水果行、菜市場、藥房等等和民
生息息相關的小店。店裡面也賣各種民生必需品。對中
國人而言，儒家就好像是開米店的，道家、佛教和西方
思想則是賣菜、賣水果的。沒有藥、沒有菜、沒有水果，
我們還能活下去；沒有米，我們就會餓死。當然，人光

　　　　吃米不夠，會營養不良，所以在歷史上也能找到中國採
　　　　用其他思想治國的例子。你所謂的新思想必須建立在傳
　　　　統的根基上，而儒家思想就是中國文化的根，根毀了，
　　　　枝葉也就凋零了。

學生：　我記得您說的例子，不過，換個角度來看，少吃米或是
　　　　偶爾改吃麵包也不錯。

教授：　我沒有理由否定你的說法。我更不是一個食古不化的人，
　　　　然而，中國走向西方，已經是無人能擋的時代潮流了。
　　　　除非你真的對西學有興趣，要不然大可不必跟著潮流跑。
　　　　看看現在的社會風氣：青少年唱英文歌、吃漢堡包；大
　　　　學生唸外文教科書、讀翻譯小說；就連專家學者發表意
　　　　見的時候，也要帶上兩句洋文，來證明自己的深度。這
　　　　樣下去，用不了五十年中國人的意識形態就會跟西方人
　　　　完全一樣。

學生：　我會再想想您的話。不過我也相信，每個時代的人都得
　　　　被迫放棄一些傳統，要是我只在一些不實際的東西上下
　　　　工夫，那不過就是浪費時間而已！對現在、對未來的中
　　　　國人都沒有好處。

教授：　「人各有志」，我不能勉強你，你也不是第一個跟我討
　　　　論這種問題的學生。無論未來的研究方向是甚麼，我都
　　　　希望你做個有良知的知識分子。

學生：　老師，也許有一天我會辜負您的期望，但是我絕不會忘
　　　　記您的教誨。

讨论题：

1. 文化是什么？请举一些例子说明。
2. 你认为什么是「中国文化」？
3. 有人喜欢分「东方文化」、「西方文化」，这个分法正确吗？
4. 我们应该怎么保存自己民族的文化？
5. 什么是「美国文化」？
6. 请说明二十世纪的文化特色。

討論題：

1. 文化是甚麼？請舉一些例子説明。
2. 你認爲甚麼是「中國文化」？
3. 有人喜歡分「東方文化」、「西方文化」，這個分法正確嗎？
4. 我們應該怎麼保存自己民族的文化？
5. 甚麼是「美國文化」？
6. 請説明二十世紀的文化特色。

【生词/生詞】

1. 一转眼 （轉）	yìzhuǎnyǎn	adv.	in the blink of an eye
2. 博士	bóshì	n.	doctor (degree)
3. 论文 （論）	lùnwén	n.	thesis
4. 文凭 （憑）	wénpíng	n.	diploma
5. 垃圾	lājī	n.	garbage
6. 儒家	rújiā	n.	the Confucianists
7. 思想	sīxiǎng	n.	thought, thinking
8. 一辈子 （輩）	yībèizi	n.	all one's life
9. 先秦	xiānqín	n.	pre-Qin Dynasty
10. 开创 （開創）	kāichuàng	v.	to start, to initiate
11. 比喻	bǐyù	n.	metaphor
12. 市场 （場）	shìchǎng	n.	market
13. 药房 （藥）	yàofáng	n.	pharmacy, drugstore
14. 民生	mínshēng	n.	people's livelihood
15. 息息相关 （關）	xīxīxiāngguān	adj.p.	(to be) closely related
16. 必需品	bìxūpǐn	n.	product of daily needs
17. 道家	dàojiā	n.	Taoism (Daoism)
18. 佛教	fójiào	n.	Buddhism
19. 饿死 （餓）	èsǐ	v.p.	to starve to death
20. 光	guāng	adv.	only
21. 采用 （採）	cǎiyòng	v.	to adopt
22. 必须 （須）	bìxū	aux.	must
23. 建立	jiànlì	v.	to establish
24. 传统 （傳統）	chuántǒng	n.	tradition
25. 根基	gēnjī	n.	foundation
26. 根	gēn	n.	root
27. 枝叶 （葉）	zhīyè	n.	leaf

28. 凋零	diāolíng	v.	to wither
39. 偶尔 （爾）	ǒu'ěr	adv.	occasionally
30. 理由	lǐyóu	n.	reason
31. 否定	fǒudìng	v.	to deny
32. 食古不化	shígǔbúhuà	adj.	(to be) pedantic
33. 挡 （擋）	dǎng	v.	to resist
34. 时代 （時）	shídài	n.	time, age, era
35. 潮流	cháoliú	n.	tide
36. 风气 （風氣）	fēngqì	n.	atmosphere
37. 浪费 （費）	làngfèi	v.	to waste
38. 志	zhì	n.	will, ideal
39. 勉强	miǎnqiǎng	v.	to force one to do ..., to be reluctant
40. 未来 （來）	wèilái	n.	future
41. 良知	liángzhī	n.	conscience
42. 知识分子 （識）	zhīshífènzǐ	n.p.	intellectual
43. 辜负 （負）	gūfù	v.	to let down
44. 期望	qīwàng	n.	expectation, hope
45. 教诲 （誨）	jiàohuì	n.	teaching, instruction

【句型】

一. 对...而言/對...而言 *adverbial phrase*: as far as ... concerned; This phrase is similar to 对...来说/對...來説; only the former is more formal.

1. 对我而言，学中文比学英文难得多。

   （對我而言，學中文比學英文難得多。）

   "To me, it is much more difficult to study Chinese than English."

2. 对有些人而言，工作不如家庭重要。

   （對有些人而言，工作不如家庭重要。）

   "To some people, work is not as important as family."

3. 对中国人而言，孝是一切道德的根本。

   （對中國人而言，孝是一切道德的根本。）

   "To Chinese people, filial piety is the basis of all morality."

二. 于.../於... *prepositional phrase*: to...

1. 他那样作于人于己都毫无用处。

   （他那樣作於人於己都毫無用處。）

   "What he does is totally useless not only to other people but also to himself."

2. 这个经济政策于国于家都没有好处。

   （這個經濟政策於國於家都沒有好處。）

   "This economic policy is not good for either the country or the family."

三. 除非...，要不然/除非...，要不然 *conjunctional phrase*: Unless... otherwise

1. 除非你真的对西学有兴趣，要不然大可不必跟著潮流跑。

   （除非你真的對西學有興趣，要不然大可不必跟著潮流跑。）

   "Unless you are really interested in Western Studies, you don't need to
   follow the current trend."

2. 除非你到中国去，要不然你吃不到地道的中国菜。

   （除非你到中國去，要不然你吃不到地道的中國菜。）

   "You cannot find authentic Chinese food to eat unless you go to China."

四. 与其... （倒）不如/與其... （倒）不如 *conjunctional phase*: better to ... than ...

    1. 与其花时间去弄那些旧东西，倒不如想办法创造新东西。

       （與其花時間去弄那些舊東西，倒不如想辦法創造新東西。）

      "It is better to create new things than to spend your time dealing with old things."

    2. 与其看电影，倒不如去跳舞。

       （與其看電影，倒不如去跳舞。）

      "It is better to go to a dance party than a movie."

五. A 和 B 息息相关/A 和 B 息息相關 *verb phrase*: A and B are closely related

    1. 国家的经济和人民的生活息息相关。

       （國家的經濟和人民的生活息息相關。）

      "The economy of the country and people's livelihood are closely related."

    2. 人民的自由和政治的发展息息相关。

       （人民的自由和政治的發展息息相關。）

      "Freedom of the people is closely related to political developments."

六. 换个角度来看/換個角度來看 *adverbial phrase*: from another perspective

    1. 名牌服装比较贵，换个角度来看，名牌服装的质量可比较好。

       （名牌服裝比較貴，換個角度來看，名牌服裝的質量可比較好。）

      "Brand-name clothes are comparatively expensive, but, on the other hand, their quality is better."

    2. 老师改我的发音让我很不好意思，不过，换个角度来看，老师也是为了我好。

       （老師改我的發音讓我很不好意思，不過，換個角度來看，老師也是為了我好。）

      "It makes me feel embarrased when the teacher corrects my pronunciation, but, looking at it from another perspective, he does that for my benefit."

七. 连...也.../連...也... *adverbial phrase*: Even ... This phrase is used to express emphasis.

1. 连专家学者发表意见的时候，也要带上两句洋文来证明自己的深度。

   （連專家學者發表意見的時候，也要帶上兩句洋文來證明自己的深度。）

   "Even when experts and scholars express their opinions, they use a few foreign sentences to show the depth of their knowledge."

2. 这么难的字连老师也不会写。

   （這麼難的字連老師也不會寫。）

   "Even teachers cannot write these kinds of difficult words."

八. 这样下去/這樣下去 *verb phrase*: to go on like this. This is a conditional clause.

1. 他每天都喝酒，这样下去，他不久就会变成一个酒鬼。

   （他每天都喝酒，這樣下去，他不久就會變成一個酒鬼。）

   "He drinks every day. If he continues like this, he will soon become a drunkard."

2. 他早起晚睡地努力工作，这样下去，他一定会得病。

   （他早起晚睡地努力工作，這樣下去，他一定會得病。）

   "He works hard-getting up early and going to bed late. If he goes on like this, he will definitely become sick."

3. 为了减肥他只吃沙拉不吃肉，这样下去，他一定会营养不良。

   （爲了減肥他只吃沙拉不吃肉，這樣下去，他一定會營養不良。）

   "To lose weight, he only eats salad and no meat. If he continues like this, he will suffer from malnutrition."

九. 不过...而已/不過...而已 *adverbial phrase*: only ...

1. 他并不是真的想骂你，不过是心情不好而已。

   （他並不是真的想罵你，不過是心情不好而已。）

   "He did not really want to scold you; he was only in a bad mood."

2. 她不是我的女朋友，我们不过是普通朋友而已。

   （她不是我的女朋友，我們不過是普通朋友而已。）

   "She is not my girlfriend; we are only friends."

【补充词汇／補充詞彙】

守旧（舊）	shǒujiù	v.	to be old-fashioned
开放（開）	kāifàng	v.	to be open
文明	wénmíng	adj./n.	(to be) civilized; civilization
人生观（觀）	rénshēngguān	n.	outlook on life
价值观（價值觀）	jiàzhíguān	n.	values
差异（異）	chāyì	n.	difference
孝顺（順）	xiàoshùn	adj.	(to be) filial
同化	tónghuà	v.	to assimilate
代沟（溝）	dàigōu	n.	generation gap
继承（繼）	jìchéng	v.	to inherit
遗产（遺產）	yíchǎn	n.	heritage
保存	bǎocún	v.	to maintain
淘汰	táotài	v.	to eliminate
个人主义（義）	gèrénzhǔyì	n.p.	individualism
全盘西化（盤）	quánpánxīhuà	v.p.	to be totally westernized
种族歧视（種，視）	zhǒngzú qíshì	n.p.	racial discrimination
取长补短（長，補）	qǔchángbǔduǎn	v.p.	to learn from others' strong points and to offset one's weakness
敬老尊贤（賢）	jìnglǎozūnxián	v.p.	to respect senior and worthy people
尊师重道（師）	zūnshīzhòngdào	v.p.	to respect one's teachers
以身作则（則）	yǐshēnzuòzé	v.p.	to use oneself as an example
以德报怨（報）	yǐdébàoyuàn	v.p.	to exchange good for evil
一毛不拔	yìmáobùbá	v.p.	to be extremely stingy
一帆风顺（風）	yìfānfēngshùn	v.p.	to be smooth all the way
不劳而获（勞，獲）	bùláo'érhuò	v.p.	to reap without sowing

〔练习〕

一. 用所给词语回答下列问题：

1. 甲：精神生活与物质生活哪个重要？（对…而言）
　　乙：

2. 甲：怎么样才能学好中文？（除非…要不然…）
　　乙：

3. 甲：你觉得创造新思想重要还是保持旧传统重要？（与其…不如…）
　　乙：

4. 甲：一个国家自由不自由跟什么有关系？（…和…息息相关）
　　乙：

5. 甲：你的中文那么好，是不是学了很多年了？（不过…而已）
　　乙：

二. 完成句子：

1. 金钱很重要，不过，换个角度来看，＿＿＿＿＿＿＿＿＿＿＿＿＿＿＿＿＿＿＿。

2. 除非你真的对西方文学有兴趣，要不然＿＿＿＿＿＿＿＿＿＿＿＿＿＿＿＿。

3. 也许我不同意你的观点，但是我绝不会＿＿＿＿＿＿＿＿＿＿＿＿＿＿＿。

4. 时间过得真快，一转眼＿＿＿＿＿＿＿＿＿＿＿＿＿＿＿＿＿＿＿＿＿。

5. 与其 _____ ，倒不如留在中国

_____ 。

三. 翻译

In order to preserve good interpersonal relations, people have to give up some of their ways of thinking. If we only pay attention to unrealistic things, then that is simply wasting time. This is harmful to both oneself and other people as well.

四. 作文：我们应该怎么保存自己民族的文化？

[練習]

一. 用所給詞語回答下列問題：

1. 甲：精神生活與物質生活哪個重要？（對...而言）

   乙：

2. 甲：怎麼樣才能學好中文？（除非...要不然...）

   乙：

3. 甲：你覺得創造新思想重要還是保持舊傳統重要？（與其...不如...）

   乙：

4. 甲：一個國家自由不自由跟甚麼有關係？（...和...息息相關）

   乙：

5. 甲：你的中文那麼好，是不是學了很多年了？（不過...而已）

   乙：

二. 完成句子

1. 金錢很重要，不過，換個角度來看，_____。

2. 除非你真的對西方文學有興趣，要不然 _____。

3. 也許我不同意你的觀點，但是我絕不會 _____。

4. 時間過得真快，一轉眼 _____。

5. 與其 _____ ，倒不如留在中國

_____ 。

三. 翻譯：

In order to preserve good interpersonal relations, people have to give up some of their ways of thinking. If we only pay attention to unrealistic things, then that is simply wasting time. This is harmful to both oneself and other people as well.

四. 作文：我們應該怎麼保存自己民族的文化？

【衍生活动】

讨论问题：小方的中国文化观

事情是这样的...

小方是个美籍留学生，在中山大学主修中国哲学。明天他要到电视公司接受「东西文化比较」节目的访问。上星期，他收到电视公司寄来的剧本，准备起来既费时又费事。现在请你帮帮忙，替他预备明天的访问。小方很爱面子，不希望自己谈话的内容太浅，因此找出了三十个不错的词汇，请你至少用十五个，回答下面的问题，千万别让小方丢脸！

小方找出的词汇：

追根究底、谦虚、孝顺、全盘西化、良知、勤奋、人道、虐待、
与人为善、吸引、采用、智慧、传宗接代、食古不化、个人主义、
敬老尊贤、尊师重道、以德报怨、知足常乐、一落千丈、价值观、
传统、落伍、报应、代沟、守旧、文明、放弃、开放、探讨

访问对话：

主持人：方先生，听说您热爱中国文化，能不能告诉观众朋友，您认为在中国文化中，哪些东西最有价值？

小方：

主持人：以您对中国的了解，您认为现代中国人怎么看待本国的传统文化？

小方：

主持人：有些人认为中国文化中某些部分已经落伍了，您觉得哪些地方应该淘汰掉？

小方：

主持人：那么，您认为西方文化里有哪些特点值得中国人学习？

小方：

【衍生活動】

討論問題：小方的中國文化觀

事情是這樣的...

　　小方是個美籍留學生，在中山大學主修中國哲學。明天他要到電視公司接受「東西文化比較」節目的訪問。上星期，他收到電視公司寄來的劇本，準備起來既費時又費事。現在請你幫幫忙，替他預備明天的訪問。小方很愛面子，不希望自己談話的內容太淺，因此找出了三十個不錯的詞彙，請你至少用十五個，回答下面的問題，千萬別讓小方丟臉！

小方找出的辭彙：

　　追根究底、謙虛、孝順、全盤西化、良知、勤奮、人道、虐待、
　　與人為善、吸引、採用、智慧、傳宗接代、食古不化、個人主義、
　　敬老尊賢、尊師重道、以德報怨、知足常樂、一落千丈、價值觀、
　　傳統、落伍、報應、代溝、守舊、文明、放棄、開放、探討

訪問對話：

主持人：方先生，聽說您熱愛中國文化，能不能告訴觀眾朋友，您認為在中國文化中，哪些東西最有價值？

小方：

主持人：以您對中國的了解，您認為現代中國人怎麼看待本國的傳統文化？

小方：

主持人：有些人認為中國文化中某些部分已經落伍了，您覺得哪些地方應該淘汰掉？

小方：

主持人：那麼，您認為西方文化裡有哪些特點值得中國人學習？

小方：

【第十二課】

快樂在哪裏？

【课文】

你快乐吗？

女儿：　妈妈，这辈子你过得快乐吗？

妈妈：　为什么问这样的问题？你觉得我不快乐吗？

女儿：　我不知道你怎么想，可是我觉得我不愿意过您那种日子。想想看，二十出头就结了婚，为家庭放弃了工作，从此与社会脱离，还不到三十就做了三个孩子的妈妈，成天不是烧饭、洗衣、整理屋子，就是给孩子换尿布、洗澡。一年三百六十五天都没有假期，没有自己的生活，只有作不完的家务事。等到年纪大了孩子也离开了，到头来只是一场空。老实说，这样的生活很难令人羡慕，也毫无快乐可言。

妈妈：　快乐是没有标准的，首先你我都同意我们之间有代沟，时代在变，人的价值观也在变，传统妇女所追求的可能正是现代妇女要摆脱的；其次，我承认我们看事情的角度不同。二十岁那年我爱上了你爸爸，那也是我的初恋，当时我觉得有情人能成眷属，就是人生最大的快乐。不久我有了孩子，现实逼得我必须在工作与家庭之间做选择，我认为陪孩子成长是千金难买的经验和快乐，于是我决定把家庭当成是一辈子的事业。孩子长大离开我是表示他们能独立地生活，我有什么不快乐的？

女儿： 可是你有没有想过家庭、儿女给你带来多大的不自由？你得牺牲和朋友跳舞、玩乐的机会，因为你的孩子应该九点准时上床睡觉。你无法安静地看书，因为孩子们的战争随时都会发生。你不能自由自在地去外地旅行，因为家里人都等着吃你的晚饭。你没办法在别的女人面前夸耀自己的事业能力，因为你的经验只限于家庭。几十年来，你辛苦地做着单调的家事，不能偷一点懒，你真的快乐吗？

妈妈： 我承认你说的都是事实，不过，人不可能什么都得到。我是失去了一些你提到的快乐，但是并不是牺牲，而是选择之后的结果。玩乐、跳舞、旅行、地位、名望，在我看来，都是属于感官的快乐，他们来得快去得也快。我所追求的是内在的快乐，这种快乐是黄金都买不到的。到目前为止，我仍然相信"拥有你所爱的，爱你所拥有的"是人生最大的快乐。

女儿： 妈妈，你说的越来越抽象，我已经听得一头雾水了。

妈妈： 举例子来说吧，晚饭的时候，看着你们大口大口地吃我作的菜，吃得津津有味，盘底朝天，我的快乐难以形容，那种感觉就像音乐家找到了知音。还有，你两岁的时候，一天清早趴在我的腿上说："妈妈，我爱你。"那种快乐足以让我忘掉生产的痛苦和带孩子的辛劳。去年参加毕业典礼，看你戴着方帽子对我微笑，我快乐得流下泪来。最后我想再提醒你一句中国的古话"知足常乐"。如果人总是在乎自己少了什么，就永远也不会快乐。

【課文】

你快樂嗎?

女兒： 媽媽，這輩子你過得快樂嗎?

媽媽： 為甚麼麼問這樣的問題? 你覺得我不快樂嗎?

女兒： 我不知道你怎麼想，可是我覺得我不願意過您那種日子。想想看，二十出頭就結了婚，為家庭放棄了工作，從此與社會脫離，還不到三十就做了三個孩子的媽媽，成天不是燒飯、洗衣、整理屋子，就是給孩子換尿布、洗澡。一年三百六十五天都沒有假期，沒有自己的生活，只有做不完的家務事。等到年紀大了孩子也離開了，到頭來只是一場空。老實說，這樣的生活很難令人羨慕，也毫無快樂可言。

媽媽： 快樂是沒有標準的，首先你我都同意我們之間有代溝，時代在變，人的價值觀也在變，傳統婦女所追求的可能正是現代婦女要擺脫的；其次，我承認我們看事情的角度不同。二十歲那年我愛上了你爸爸，那也是我的初戀，當時我覺得有情人能成眷屬，就是人生最大的快樂。不久我有了孩子，現實逼得我必須在工作與家庭之間做選擇，我認為陪孩子成長是千金難買的經驗和快樂，於是我決定把家庭當成是一輩子的事業。孩子長大離開我是表示他們能獨立地生活，我有甚麼不快樂的?

女兒： 可是你有沒有想過家庭、兒女給你帶來多大的不自由？
你得犧牲和朋友跳舞、玩樂的機會，因為你的孩子應該
九點準時上牀睡覺。你無法安靜地看書，因為孩子們的
戰爭隨時都會發生。你不能自由自在地去外地旅行，因
為家裏人都等着吃你的晚飯。你沒辦法在別的女人面前
誇耀自己的事業能力，因為你的經驗只限於家庭。幾十
年來，你辛苦地做着單調的家事，不能偷一點懶，你真
的快樂嗎？

媽媽： 我承認你說的都是事實，不過，人不可能甚麼都得到。
我是失去了一些你提到的快樂，但是並不是犧牲，而是
選擇之後的結果。玩樂、跳舞、旅行、地位、名望，在
我看來，都是屬於感官的快樂，他們來得快去得也快。
我所追求的是內在的快樂，這種快樂是黃金都買不到的。
到目前為止，我仍然相信"擁有你所愛的，愛你所擁有
的"是人生最大的快樂。

女兒： 媽媽，你說的越來越抽象，我已經聽得一頭霧水了。

媽媽： 舉例子來說吧，晚飯的時候，看着你們大口大口地吃我
做的菜，吃得津津有味，盤底朝天，我的快樂難以形容，
那種感覺就像音樂家找到了知音。還有，你兩歲的時候，
一天清早趴在我的腿上說："媽媽，我愛你。"那種快
樂足以讓我忘掉生產的痛苦和帶孩子的辛勞。去年參加
畢業典禮，看你戴着方帽子對我微笑，我快樂得流下淚
來。最後我想再提醒你一句中國的古話"知足常樂"。
如果人總是在乎自己少了甚麼，就永遠也不會快樂。

讨论题：

    1. 在你的经验里，什么是最快乐的事？

    2. 以你的标准，你认为妈妈的生活快乐吗？

    3. 你希望你的女儿成为家庭妇女还是职业妇女？为什么？

    4. "知足常乐"这个观念会不会影响社会进步？为什么？

    5. 金钱能不能买到快乐？

    6. 你不快乐的时候，用什么方法让自己快乐？

討論題：

    1. 在你的經驗裏，甚麼是最快樂的事？

    2. 以你的標準，你認為媽媽的生活快樂嗎？

    3. 你希望你的女兒成爲家庭婦女還是職業婦女？爲甚麼？

    4. "知足常樂"這個觀念會不會影響社會進步？爲甚麼？

    5. 金錢能不能買到快樂？

    6. 你不快樂的時候，用甚麼方法讓自己快樂？

【生词/生詞】

1. 快乐 （樂）	kuàilè	adj./n.	(to be) happy, happiness
2. 出头 （頭）	chūtóu	prep.	over (20 years old)
3. 成天	chéngtiān	adv.	all day long
4. 尿布	niàobù	n.	diaper
5. 到头来 （頭）	dàotóulái	adv.p.	in the end
6. 标准 （標準）	biāozhǔn	n.	standard
7. 代沟 （溝）	dàigōu	n.	generation gap
8. 价值观 （價、觀）	jiàzhíguān	n.	outlook, value concept
9. 追求	zhuīqiú	v./n.	to pursue; chase
10. 摆脱 （擺）	bǎituō	v.	to get rid of
11. 承认 （認）	chéngrèn	v.	to admit
12. 角度	jiǎodù	n.	angle, perspective
13. 爱上了 （愛）	àishàngle	v.p	to fall in love with...
14. 眷属 （屬）	juànshǔ	n.	family members
15. 千金难买 （難買）	qiānjīnnánmǎi	adj.p.	difficult to obtain with a lot of gold
16. 独立 （獨）	dúlì	adj./n.	(to be) independent; independence
17. 牺牲 （犧）	xīshēng	v./n.	to sacrifice; sacrifice
18. 安静	ānjìng	adj.	(to be) quiet
19. 夸耀 （誇）	kuāyào	v.	to praise
20. 限于 （於）	xiànyú	v.	to be limited to
21. 单调 （單調）	dāndiào	adj.	(to be) monotonous
22. 偷懒 （懶）	tōulǎn	v.	to loaf on the job
23. 地位	dìwèi	n.	status
24. 名望	míngwàng	n.	reputation
25. 属于 （屬於）	shǔyú	v.	to belong to

26. 内在	nèizài	adj.	(to be) internal
27. 黄金（黃）	huángjīn	n.	(yellow) gold
28. 拥有（擁）	yōngyǒu	v.	to own
29. 抽象	chōuxiàng	adj.	(to be) abstract
30. 一头雾水（頭霧）	yìtóuwùshuǐ	adj.p.	to be totally confused
31. 津津有味	jīnjīnyǒuwèi	adv.p.	with great pleasure
32. 知音	zhīyīn	n.	close friend
33. 辛劳（勞）	xīnláo	n.	hard labor/work
34. 典礼（禮）	diǎnlǐ	n.	ceremony
35. 微笑	wēixiào	n.	smile
36. 知足常乐（樂）	zhīzúchánglè	v.p.	One is always happy if content with one's lot.

【句型】

一. 与...脱离（关系）/與...脱離（關係） *verb phrase*: to separate oneself from ...

　　1. 你愿意不愿意为家庭放弃工作，与社会脱离？

　　（你願意不願意為家庭放棄工作，與社會脱離？）

　　"Are you willing to give up work for your family and stay away from society?"

　　2. 由于政见不同，他决定与父母脱离关系。你会这样作吗？

　　（由於政見不同，他決定與父母脱離關係。你會這樣作嗎？）

　　"Because of different political viewpoints, he has decided to break off relations with his parents. Would you do that?"

二. 还不到 + time phrase 就.../還不到 + time phrase 就... *adverbial phrase*: as early as...; This structure is used to emphasize that something happened as early as ...

　　1. 还不到三十她就做了三个孩子的妈妈。

（還不到三十她就做了三個孩子的媽媽。）

"She became a mother of three children even before the age of 30."

2. 还不到二十岁他就大学毕业了，人们都说他是个神童。

（還不到二十歲他就大學畢業了，人們都説他是個神童。）

"He graduated from college before the age of 20; people called him a child of rare talent."

3. 还不到两个星期他就爱上了她。

（還不到兩個星期他就愛上了她。）

"He fell in love with her in less than two weeks."

三. 不是...就是/不是...就是 *conjunction*: either... or ...

1. 每个周末他们不是喝啤酒就是跳舞，从来不学习。

（每個週末他們不是喝啤酒就是跳舞，從來不學習。）

"Every weekend they either drink beer or dance, but they never study."

2. 不是病了就是功课太多，要不然他不会不来。

（不是病了就是功課太多，要不然他不會不來。）

"He is either sick or has too much homework, otherwise he would be here."

四. 等到/等到 + time phrase or clause. *verb phrase*: to wait until...

1. 等到年纪大了孩子也离开了。

（等到年紀大了孩子也離開了。）

"By the time they were old, all of the children had left."

2. 年轻的时候他没有钱去旅行，可是等到钱多了他也老了。

（年輕的時候他沒有錢去旅行，可是等到錢多了他也老了。）

"He did not have money to travel when he was young, and by the time he had money, he was old."

五. 令人羡慕/令人羨慕 *verb phrase*: to make people envious. There are many other combinations of this kind such as: 令人满意、令人鼓舞、令人敬佩、令人深思等。

1. 他刚毕业就找到了一个很好的工作，的确令人羡慕。

（他剛畢業就找到了一個很好的工作，的確令人羨慕。）

"He found a very good job as soon as he graduated, which really made people envy him."

2. 他常常提出一些令人深思的問題。

（他常常提出一些令人深思的問題。）

"He often raises questions that make people think deeply."

六. 在...与...之间做选择/在...與...之間做選擇 *verb phrase*: to make a choice between ... and ...

1. 在工作与家庭之间做选择不是一件很容易的事。

（在工作與家庭之間做選擇不是一件很容易的事。）

"It is not easy to make a choice between work and family."

2. 很多申请这个工作的人是我的朋友，我不知道如何在他们之间做选择。

（很多申請這個工作的人是我的朋友，我不知道如何在他們之間做選擇。）

"Many of the people who applied for this job are my friends. I don't know how to make a choice among them."

七. 到目前为止/到目前為止 *adverbial phrase*: as of now, up to now, to this day

1. 到目前为止我还不知道美国的大城市为什么有那么多无家可归的人。

（到目前為止我還不知道美國的大城市為甚麼有那麼多無家可歸的人。）

"Up to this point, I still don't understand why there are so many homeless people in big cities of the United States."

2. 到目前为止，她一直认为人生最大的快乐是有情人能成眷属。

（到目前為止，她一直認為人生最大的快樂是有情人能成眷屬。）

"Up to now, she has always believed that the most enjoyable thing in life is to marry someone whom one really loves."

八. 难以/難以 + disyllabic verb. *verb phrase*: to be difficult to ...; This phrase is often used in 书面语/書面語 shūmiànyǔ (written/formal language). The following are some commonly-used combinations: 难以形容/難以形容、难以想像/難以想像、难以忍受/難以忍受、难以对付/难以对付，等。

1. 留学八年回国与家人团聚，他说当时的快乐难以形容。

   （留學八年回國與家人團聚，他説當時的快樂難以形容。）

   "He returned to his home country for a reunion with his family after eight years of studying abroad. He said it was difficult to describe how happy he was at that time."

2. 文革期间他忍受的痛苦是难以想像的。

   （文革期間他忍受的痛苦是難以想像的。）

   "It is difficult to imagine the suffering he endured during the Cultural Revolution."

【语法/語法】

能愿动词/能願動詞
(Auxiliary/Helping Verbs)

Auxiliary verbs, or helping verbs, differ from regular verbs in that they cannot be used independently, but must be used with regular verbs. There are many auxiliary verbs in Chinese; however, in this lesson we only focus on a few of the most commonly used ones and make distinctions among them. In general, Chinese grammarians divide auxiliary verbs into two categories: one includes those that express willingness, such as 要, 想, 愿意/願意, 应/應, 该/該, 能, 可以, 得, etc.; the other includes those that express either ablility or possiblity, such as （可）能, 可以, 会/會, 得, etc. Let us look at some examples:

1. 我妹妹要去中国结婚。/我妹妹要去中國結婚。

   "My sister wants to go to China to get married."

   (She has a strong desire to do so.)

2. 我妹妹想去中国结婚。/我妹妹想去中國結婚。

   "My sister wants to go to China to get married."

   (The desire to do so is not as strong as in sentence 1.)

3. 我妹妹愿意去中国结婚。/我妹妹願意去中國結婚。

"My sister is willing to go to China to get married."

(If someone asks her to do so.)

4. 我妹妹可以去中国结婚。/我妹妹可以去中國結婚。

"My sister could go to China to get married." (If it is necessary.)

5. 我妹妹可能去中国结婚。/我妹妹可能去中國結婚。

"It is possible that my sister will go to China to get married."

(But it is not certain yet.)

6. 我妹妹能去中国结婚。/我妹妹能去中國結婚。

"My sister can go to China to get married." (Implies that my sister has the ablity of doing this, and this ablity is stronger than that in 4. However, whether she will do that or not is a different matter.)

7. 我妹妹应该去中国结婚。/我妹妹應該去中國結婚。

"My sister should go to China to get married."

(Implies that she should not get married in any other place.)

8. 我妹妹会去中国结婚。/我妹妹會去中國結婚。

"My sister will go to China to get married."

(Implies that she IS going and she knows how to go there.)

9. 我妹妹得去中国结婚。/我妹妹得去中國結婚。

"My sister has to go to China to get married."

(Implies that there is no other choice.)

From the above examples, we see that all the auxiliary verbs can express either willingness and/or ablility/possiblity; however, they express different degrees of willingness, ablility, and possiblity, which can be illustrated by the following hierarchy:

Willingness:得 〈应该/應該 〈可以 〈想 〈会/會 〈愿意/願意 〈要

Ablility:　　可以 〈会/會 〈能

Possiblity: 应该/應該 〈可以 〈可能 〈会/會 〈要 〈得

The degree of willingness, ablility, or possiblity is lowest on the left-most side and highest on the right-most side. For instance, if one says: 我得去, it means, "I really don't want to go, but I have to go;" whereas if one says: 我要去, it means, "I really want to go." Similarly, 我应该/應該去 means "Yes, I should go (but in my mind there is no chance for me to go)." In comparison, 我得去 means, "I definitely will go (because I have the obligation to do so)."

【补充词汇/補充詞彙】

欢喜 （歡）	huānxǐ	v.	to be delighted
激动 （動）	jīdòng	v.	to be excited
感激	gǎnjī	v.	to feel grateful
笑	xiào	v.	to laugh
微笑	wēixiào	v.	to smile
大笑	dàxiào	v.	to laugh loudly
爱好 （愛）	àihào	v.	to be fond of
满意 （滿）	mǎnyì	v.	to be satisfied
得到满足	dédào mǎnzú	v.p.	to obtain satisfaction
感到满意	gǎndào mǎnyì	v.p.	to feel satisfied
使...满意	shǐ ... mǎnyì	v.p.	to make ... satisfied
追求享受	zhuīqiú xiǎngshòu	v.p.	to pursue enjoyment
取乐 （樂）	qǔlè	v.p.	to obtain happiness
运气 （運氣）	yùnqì	n.	luck

【练习】

一. 用所给词语回答问题：

1. 你打算什么时候结婚，建立自己的家庭？ 〔等到 + time ..., 老实说〕

2. 如果你需要在家庭和事业之间作选择，你会怎么办？ 〔会，令人羡慕，放弃〕

3. 知足常乐的观念会不会影响社会的进步？ 〔难以..., 与 ...脱离〕

二. 选词填空：

> 有了...就有了...、值得、为...牺牲...、就...、
> 在...看来、毫无兴趣、千金难买、但是

　　什么是快乐？我想每个人的快乐观都不一样。有的人觉得赚钱最快乐，
_____ 钱 _____ 一切，他们可以 _____ 赚钱 _____ 家庭或者朋
友。 _____ 有的人对金钱 _____ ，他们认为钱多钱少跟快乐毫无关系，
成天为了钱精打细算，辛辛苦苦不 _____ 。 _____ 他们 _____ ，家
庭朋友最重要，建立一个美好的家庭，是 _____ 的快乐。还有一些人认为
自由最令人羡慕，一个人想作什么 _____ 作什么，才是真正的快乐。

三. 用中文解释下列词组：

1. 知足常乐

2. 千金难买

3. 价值观

4. 代沟

四. 作文：谈谈你认为最快乐的事 (The composition should consist of both general statements and supporting details).

【練習】

一. 用所給詞語回答問題：

1. 你打算甚麼時候結婚，建立自己的家庭？ （等到 + time..., 老實説）

2. 如果你需要在家庭和事業之間作選擇，你會怎麼辦？ （會，令人羨慕，放棄）

3. 知足常樂的觀念會不會影響社會的進步？ （難以..., 與 ...脫離）

二. 選詞填空：

> 有了...就有了...、值得、為...犧牲...、就...、
> 在...看來、毫無興趣、千金難買、但是

甚麼是快樂？我想每個人的快樂觀都不一樣。有的人覺得賺錢最快樂，
＿＿＿＿＿錢＿＿＿＿＿一切，他們可以＿＿＿＿＿賺錢＿＿＿＿＿家庭或者朋
友。＿＿＿＿＿有的人對金錢＿＿＿＿＿，他們認為錢多錢少跟快樂毫無關係，
成天為了錢精打細算，辛辛苦苦不＿＿＿＿＿。＿＿＿＿＿他們＿＿＿＿＿，家庭
朋友最重要，建立一個美好的家庭，是＿＿＿＿＿的快樂。還有一些人認為自
由最令人羨慕，一個人想作甚麼＿＿＿＿＿作甚麼，才是真正的快樂。

三. 用中文解釋下列詞組：

1. 知足常樂

2. 千金難買

3. 價值觀

4. 代溝

四. 作文：談談你認為最快樂的事 (The composition should consist of both general statements and supporting details).

【衍生活动】

翻译与讨论

请用你的母语翻译下列各句，并选出五个你认为最快乐的情况和老师同学分享你的经验。

1. 和心爱的人一同观赏落日
2. 在公用电话的退币口捡到钱
3. 老婆（公）说你苗条了
4. 回到家发现有一束花在门口等你
5. 一家人团聚吃年夜饭。
6. 赶上截止日期
7. 考试拿满分
8. 拍出一张自己很满意的照片
9. 打赌赢了
10. 老板给你加薪
11. 初吻
12. 情人节有男（女）友陪伴
13. 偿还了最后一笔学生助学贷款
14. 在外套口袋里发现去年冬天遗忘的钱
15. 好书看到精彩处

【衍生活動】

翻譯與討論

請用母語翻譯下列各句，並選出五個你認爲最快樂的情況和老師同學分享你的經驗。

1. 和心愛的人一同觀賞落日
2. 在公用電話的退幣口撿到錢
3. 老婆（公）說你苗條了
4. 回到家發現有一束花在門口等你
5. 一家人團聚吃年夜飯
6. 趕上截止日期
7. 考試拿滿分
8. 拍出一張自己很滿意的照片
9. 打賭贏了
10. 老闆給你加薪
11. 初吻
12. 情人節有男（女）友陪伴
13. 償還了最後一筆學生助學貸款
14. 在外套口袋裡發現去年冬天遺忘的錢
15. 好書看到精彩處

【第十三課】

選舉

【课文】

选举

老陈： 一大早就无精打采的，是不是周末玩儿过头了？

老林： 什么玩儿过头了，昨天我可是尽了好市民的义务，一整天参加了三个市长候选人举办的竞选活动。早上是执政党的"爱国家升旗典礼"，下午是在野党的"反贪污万人大游行"，晚上则是第三党的"环保歌唱之夜"，一连串的活动从早上七点到晚上十点，你说我累不累？

老陈： 结论如何？找到理想的候选人没有？

老林： 其实这三位候选人的政见，都在媒体上刊登、发表过，没什么新鲜的，唯一让我大开眼界的是群众的反应。参加活动的群众太热情、太偏激，几乎已经到了丧失理性的地步。在那种情况下让人心中产生一种相当不安的感觉。难道这就是推行民主政治的结果？如果民主真是如此，那民主跟毒品、宗教狂热就相去不远了。

老陈： 你这几年在国外念书，可能不太清楚最近的选举文化。以往那种挨家挨户访问，握手寒暄的拉票方式已经落伍了，取而代之的是搞群众运动，煽动族群对立，为了胜利不惜使用暴力、抹黑、造谣、分化、贿赂等手段。一个月来，报纸上五分之四的篇幅都在报道选情，群众的情绪已经被激到了最高点。昨天我太太还为了支持不同的候选人跟我大吵了一架，再下去准会有人因为选举离婚。

老林：　以目前的选举狂热看来，这次的投票率可能会打破以往的记录。记得小时候，每次选举前政府总是积极鼓励人民去投票，选举后也会公布投票率，好像投票率越高国家就越民主似的。不过，世界上真正实行民主的国家投票率并不高，能有百分之五十就不错了。投票率跟民主化的程度到底有没有必然关系实在很难说。

老陈：　投票率太高也可能是社会动乱的征兆。你想想看，如果一个国家的政情稳定，人民在政治上有共识，无论那个党执政，基本国策都不会有太大的改变，如此一来，人民投票的动机一定不高。反之，要是一国之内，执政党跟在野党的目标完全不同，群众为了拥护和自己政见一致的候选人，就会积极投入选举，那么投票率自然会提高许多。当投票率超过百分之九十的时候，动乱可能就不远了。

老林：　但愿我们是杞人忧天。现在我只希望选举后一切能恢复正常，让老百姓安稳地过日子。

讨论题：

1. 你用什么标准来决定给谁投票？
2. 投票率跟民主化的程度有没有关系？为什么？
3. 在你看来民主制度有哪些优点和缺点？
4. 现在的社会里什么样的人掌握政权？中产阶级？大企业家？政客？
5. 你认为资本主义跟民主政治有什么关系？
6. 为什么有人说"政治是高明的骗术"？
7. 假如你是市长候选人，请发表你的政见。

【課文】

選舉

老陳： 一大早就無精打采的，是不是週末玩兒過頭了？

老林： 甚麼玩兒過頭了，昨天我可是盡了好市民的義務，一整天參加了三個市長候選人舉辦的競選活動。早上是執政黨的"愛國家升旗典禮"，下午是在野黨的"反貪污萬人大遊行"，晚上則是第三黨的"環保歌唱之夜"，一連串的活動從早上七點到晚上十點，你說我累不累？

老陳： 結論如何？找到理想的候選人沒有？

老林： 其實這三位候選人的政見，都在媒體上刊登、發表過，沒甚麼新鮮的，唯一讓我大開眼界的是羣眾的反應。參加活動的羣眾太熱情、太偏激，幾乎已經到了喪失理性的地步。在那種情況下讓人心中產生一種相當不安的感覺。難道這就是推行民主政治的結果？如果民主真是如此，那民主跟毒品、宗教狂熱就相去不遠了。

老陳： 你這幾年在國外唸書，可能不太清楚最近的選舉文化。以往那種挨家挨戶訪問，握手寒喧的拉票方式已經落伍了，取而代之的是搞羣眾運動，煽動族羣對立，為了勝利不惜使用暴力、抹黑、造謠、分化、賄賂等手段。一個月來，報紙上五分之四的篇幅都在報道選情，羣眾的情緒已經被激到了最高點。昨天我太太還為了支持不同的候選人跟我大吵了一架，再下去準會有人因為選舉離婚。

老林： 以目前的選舉狂熱看來，這次的投票率可能會打破以往的記錄。記得小時候，每次選舉前政府總是積極鼓勵人民去投票，選舉後也會公布投票率，好像投票率越高國家就越民主似的。不過，世界上真正實行民主的國家投票率並不高，能有百分之五十就不錯了。投票率跟民主化的程度到底有沒有必然關係實在很難說。

老陳： 投票率太高也可能是社會動亂的徵兆。你想想看，如果一個國家的政情穩定，人民在政治上有共識，無論那個黨執政，基本國策都不會有太大的改變，如此一來，人民投票的動機一定不高。反之，要是一國之內，執政黨跟在野黨的目標完全不同，羣眾為了擁護和自己政見一致的候選人，就會積極投入選舉，那麼投票率自然會提高許多。當投票率超過百分之九十的時候，動亂可能就不遠了。

老林： 但願我們是杞人憂天。現在我只希望選舉後一切能恢復正常，讓老百姓安穩地過日子。

討論題：
1. 你用甚麼標準來決定給誰投票？
2. 投票率跟民主化的程度有沒有關係？為甚麼？
3. 在你看來民主制度有哪些優點和缺點？
4. 現在的社會裏甚麼樣的人掌握政權？中產階級？大企業家？政客？
5. 你認為資本主義跟民主政治有甚麼關係？
6. 為甚麼有人說"政治是高明的騙術"？
7. 假如你是市長候選人，請發表你的政見。

【生词/生詞】

1. 选举（選舉） xuǎnjǔ v./n. to elect; election
2. 无精打采（無） wújīngdǎcǎi v.p. to be spiritless
3. 义务（義務） yìwù n. obligation
4. 候选人（選） hòuxuǎnrén n. candidate
5. 举办（舉辦） jǔbàn v. to hold (e.g. meeting)
6. 竞选（競選） jìngxuǎn v. to run for office
7. 活动（動） huódòng n. activity
8. 执政党（執黨） zhízhèngdǎng n. party in office
9. 在野党（黨） zàiyědǎng n. party not in office
10. 反 fǎn v. to oppose
11. 贪污（貪） tānwū n./v. embezzlement; to embezzle
12. 游行（遊） yóuxíng v./n. to parade; parade
13. 环保（環） huánbǎo n. environmental protection
14. 一连串（連） yìliánchuàn n. a series of
15. 结论（結論） jiélùn n. conclusion
16. 理想 lǐxiǎng n. ideal
17. 其实（實） qíshí adv. actually
18. 政见（見） zhèngjiàn n. political viewpoints
19. 媒体（體） méitǐ n. media
20. 刊登 kāndēng v. to publish (e.g. newspapers)
21. 新鲜（鮮） xīnxiān adj. (to be) fresh
22. 唯一 wéiyī adj. only
23. 热情（熱） rèqíng adj. (to be) kind, enthusiastic
24. 偏激 piānjī adj. (to be) extreme
25. 丧失（喪） sàngshī v. to lose
26. 理性 lǐxìng n. ration
27. 产生（產） chǎnshēng v. to produce, to come into being
28. 推行 tuīxíng v. to implement, to carry out

29. 民主	mínzhǔ	adj./n.	democratic; democracy
30. 政治	zhèngzhì	n.	politics
31. 结果	jiéguǒ	n.	result
32. 握手	wòshǒu	v.p.	shake hands
33. 寒喧	hánxuān	v.	to chat
34. 拉票	lāpiào	v.p	to solicit votes
35. 方式	fāngshì	n.	style
36. 落伍	luòwǔ	v.	to fall behind
37. 取而代之	qǔ'érdàizhī	v.p.	to substitute
38. 煽动（動）	shāndòng	v.	to instigate
39. 暴力	bàolì	n.	violence
40. 造谣（謠）	zàoyáo	v.	to spread rumors
41. 分化	fēnhuà	v.	to split up
42. 贿赂（賄賂）	huìlù	v.	to bribe
43. 手段	shǒuduàn	n.	measure, means
44. 报道（報）	bàodào	v./n.	to report; report
45. 情绪（緒）	qíngxù	n.	mood, feeling
46. 吵架	chǎojià	v./n.	to quarrel; quarrel
47. 率	lǜ	n.	ratio
48. 积极（積極）	jījí	adj.	(to be) active
49. 鼓励（勵）	gǔlì	v./n.	to encourage; encouragement
50. 公布	gōngbù	v.	to announce
51. 不过（過）	búguò	adv.	however
52. 实行（實）	shíxíng	v.	to carry out (policy)
53. 动乱（動亂）	dòngluàn	n.	disturbance, turmoil
54. 征兆（徵）	zhèngzhào	n.	sign
55. 稳定（穩）	wěndìng	adj.	(to be) stable
56. 动机（動機）	dòngjī	n.	motivation
57. 拥护（擁護）	yōnghù	v.	to support
58. 投入	tóurù	v.	to throw oneself into
59. 杞人忧天（憂）	qǐrényōutiān	v.p.	to be always worried
60. 安稳（穩）	ānwěn	adj.	(to be) smooth and steady

【句型】

一. 在...情况下/在...情況下 *adverbial phrase*: under the circumstance of..., in the event of...

    1. 在经济不景气的情况下物价会发生什么变化？

    （在經濟不景氣的情況下物價會發生甚麼變化？）

  "In the event of a sluggish economy, what would happen to prices?"

    2. 在还没有看到他的情况下，我不会说什么。

    （在還沒有看到他的情況下，我不會說甚麼。）

  "Before I see him, I will not say anything."

二. 跟... 相去不远/跟... 相去不遠 *verb phrase*: to be almost the same as...; This phrase is much more formal in style than 跟...差不多一样/跟...差不多一樣.

    1. 他虽然是共和党，但是他跟民主党人的政见相去不远。

    （他雖然是共和黨，但是他跟民主黨人的政見相去不遠。）

  "Although he is a Republican, his political viewpoints are almost the same as those of the Democrats."

    2. 那些参加选举活动的群众太偏激了，跟宗教狂热已经相去不远。

    （那些參加選舉活動的羣眾太偏激了，跟宗教狂熱已經相去不遠。）

  "Those people participated in the election to such an extreme degree that they were almost the same as religious fanatics."

三. 以往/以往 *adverbial phrase*: before, in the past; This phrase indicates a time contrast between the past and the present. (It may imply that somone is no longer doing something.)

    1. 她以往对政治很热心，而今她对政治毫无兴趣。

    （她以往對政治很熱心，而今他對政治毫無興趣。）

  "She used to be enthusiastic about politics, but now she is no longer interested."

    2. 他以往上课总是无精打采，可是现在每节课他都很积极。

（他以往上課總是無精打採，可是現在每節課他都很積極。）

"He used to be spiritless in class, but now he is actively involved in every class."

四. 以...看来/以...看來 *adverbial phrase*: judging from ... (we can infer)

1. 以现在的情况看来，美国的经济最近几年会有什么变化？

（以現在的情況看來，美國的經濟最近幾年會有甚麼變化？）

"Judging from the current situation, what changes may happen to the economy of the United States in the next few years?"

2. 以他的长相来看，他是一个很严肃的人。

（以他的長相來看，他是一個很嚴肅的人。）

"Judging from his appearance, he is a very serious person."

五. 打破...的记录/打破...的記錄 *verb phrase*: to break the record of...

1. 她连续三年打破了一千米长跑的记录。

（她連續三年打破了一千米長跑的記錄。）

"She has broken the record in the 1000 meter run each year for the last three consecutive years."

2. 今年参加选举的人数已经打破了以往的记录。

（今年參加選舉的人數已經打破了以往的記錄。）

"This year the number of people participating in the election has broken the record."

六. 到底/到底 *adverbial phrase*: indeed, really; This phrase makes the tone of questioning more emphatic.

1. 你到底参加不参加今年的选举？

（你到底參加不參加今年的選舉？）

"Are you going to vote this year or not?"

2. 喝酒到底能不能解愁？

（喝酒到底能不能解愁？）

"Does drinking really help to eleminate one's worries?"

七. 跟...有关系/跟...有關係 *verb phrase*: to be related to ..., to be associated with ...

　　1. 一个人钱多少跟他快乐不快乐到底有没有关系？

　　　 （一個人錢多少跟他快樂不快樂到底有沒有關係？）

　　　 "Does one's happiness really depend on the amount of money one has?"

　　2. 投票率跟民主化的程度到底有没有必然关系实在很难说。

　　　 （投票率跟民主化的程度到底有沒有必然關係實在很難說。）

　　　 "It is hard to say whether the number of people participating in the election is
　　　 related to the degree of democracy."

　　3. 毕业以后能不能找到好工作跟什么有关系？

　　　 （畢業以後能不能找到好工作跟甚麼有關係？）

　　　 "What determines whether or not you will find a good job after graduation?"

八. 无论... 都.../無論... 都... *conjunction*: no matter ...; What follows the word 无论 is
a type of question such as 1) A Not A, 2) A or B, 3) wh-question.

　　1. 无论她爱不爱他，她都得听从父母之命，跟他结婚。

　　　 （無論她愛不愛他，她都得聽從父母之命，跟他結婚。）

　　　 "Whether she loves him or not, she will have to listen to her parents and marry
　　　 him."

　　2. 无论总统是共和党还是民主党，老百姓的生活过得都是一样的。

　　　 （無論總統是共和黨還是民主黨，老百姓的生活過得都是一樣的。）

　　　 "It does not matter whether the President is a Republican or a Democrat; the
　　　 common people will live the same life as before."

　　3. 无论哪个党执政，基本国策都不会有太大的改变。

　　　 （無論哪個黨執政，基本國策都不會有太大的改變。）

　　　 "No matter which party is in power, the basic policies of the country will be
　　　 more or less the same."

【语法/語法】

句子连接词/句子連接詞
(Sentence Linking Words)

By now, students should have learned many Chinese linking words that are used to connect sentences. Therefore, this section on grammatical notes is designed to give a brief summary of the functions of linking words. Generally speaking, there are two types of linking words in Chinese: one type is used to connect sentences in the immediately following discourse (henceforth Type 1), the other is used to connect sentences in the immediately preceding discourse (henceforth Type 2). Among Type 1 linking words, some can be positioned either after the topic/subject or in sentence-initial position, others can only be positioned in sentence final position. By comparison, most Type 2 linking words are positioned either in sentence-initial position or after the topic/subject. For instance:

1. 他来的时候，我正在看电视。/他來的時候，我正在看電視。
   (Type 1 linking word) "When he came, I was watching TV."
2. 如果你同意，我马上跟你结婚。/如果你同意，我馬上跟你結婚。
   (Type 1 linking word) "If you agree, I will marry you right away."
3. 他不想学中文，但是他想去中国。/他不想學中文，但是他想去中國。
   (Type 2 linking word)

   "He does not want to study Chinese, but he wants to go to China."

Notice that Chinese linking words are not equivalent to English conjunctions; they can be either a combination of nominal+noun (as in 1), a conjunction (as in 2), or an adverb (as in 3). Students may have noticed that many Type 1 linking words co-occur with Type 2, as exemplified below:

4. 他不但是我的父亲，而且是我的好朋友。
   他不但是我的父親，而且是我的好朋友。)
   "He is not only my father, but also my good friend."
5. 奇怪的是我一来，他就走。
   奇怪的是我一來，他就走。
   "It is strange that as soon as I came, he left."

It should be pointed out that Type 2 linking words cannot be positioned after the topic unless it occurs together with a Type 1 linking word. In other words, 但是 in 3 cannot be positioned after the topic pronoun 他, whereas 就 in 5 can and must be positioned after the topic.

As far as the semantics of Chinese linking words are concerned, they can convey numerous meanings: time, cause, result, concession, condition, listing, contrast, transition, etc. For instance:

6. 要是你不来，请告诉我一下。
   要是你不來，請告訴我一下。 (condition)

   "If you will not come, please let me know."

7. 她又漂亮又聪明。/她又漂亮又聰明。 (listing)

   "She is not only pretty, but also smart."

8. 虽然他脾气不好，但是他很愿意帮助别人。
   雖然他脾氣不好，但是他很願意幫助別人。 (contrast, transition)

   "Although he has a bad temper, he is willing to help others."

9. 除非他给我道歉，我才跟他说话。
   除非他給我道歉，我才跟他說話。 (concession)

   "I will talk to him only if he apologizes."

10. 因为他是我的老师，所以我很尊敬他。
    因爲他是我的老師，所以我很尊敬他。 (cause & result)

    "I respect him because he is my teacher."

The following table provides a brief summary of the most commonly used linking words in Chinese:

Chinese Linking Words		Gloss	Type 1/2
并且	bìngqiě	moreover	2
不但	búdàn...	not only	1
不过 (過)	búguò	not/however	2
不论 (論)	búlùn	no matter	1
除非	chúfēi	unless	1
但是	dànshì	but/nevertheless	1
的话 (話)	...de huà	if	1
的时候 (時)	...de shíhòu	when	1

而且	érqiě	but also	2
还是 （還）	háishì	or	2
或是	huòshì	or	2
或者	huòzhě	or	2
假如	jiǎrú...	if	1
假使	jiǎshǐ	even if	1
既然	jìrán	since	1
即使	jíshǐ...	even if	1
可是	kěshì	but/however	2
然而	rán'ér	however	2
如果	rúguǒ...	if	1
省得	shěngde	so as to avoid	2
虽然 （雖）	suīrán...	although	1
所以	suǒyǐ	therefore	2
为的是 （爲）	wèideshì	for/in order to	2
无论 （論）	wúlùn	no matter whether	1
要不是	yàobúshì	if not that	2
要是	yàoshì	if	1
一...就	yī...jiù...	as soon as	1
以后 （後）	yǐhòu	after	1
以前	yǐqián	before	1
因为 （爲）	yīnwèi...	because/since	1
由于 （於）	yóuyú...	because	1
又...又	yòu...yòu	not only...but also	1&2
越...越	yuè...yuè	the more...the more	1&2
只要	zhǐyào...	if only/as long as	1
只有	zhǐyǒu...	only when	1

【补充词汇/補充詞彙】

国务院（國務）	guówùyuàn	n.	the State Concil
委员会（員會）	wěiyuánhuì	n.	committee
共产党（產黨）	gòngchǎndǎng	n.	Communist Party
国民党（國、黨）	guómíndǎng	n.	Nationalist Party
民主党（黨）	mínzhǔdǎng	n.	Democratic Party
共和党（黨）	gònghédǎng	n.	Republican Party
主席	zhǔxí	n.	chairman
总理（總）	zǒnglǐ	n.	prime minister (China)
首相	shǒuxiàng	n.	prime minister (Japan)
部长（長）	bùzhǎng	n.	minister
选举人（選舉）	xuǎnjǔrén	n.	elector
竞选伙伴（競選）	jìngxuǎn huǒbàn	n.	running-mate
左派	zuǒpài	n.	left wing
右派	yòupài	n.	right wing
总统（總統）	zǒngtǒng	n.	president (US)
国务卿（國務）	guówùqīng	n.	secretary of state (US)
众议院（眾議）	zhòngyìyuàn	n.	speaker of the house (US)
众议员（眾議員）	zhòngyìyuán	n.	house representative (US)
参议院（參議）	cānyìyuàn	n.	senate (US)
参议员（參議員）	cānyìyuán	n.	senator
负责（負責）	fùzé	v.	to be in charge of ...
投票	tóupiào	v.	to vote for ...
赞成（贊）	zànchéng	v.	to endorse
反对（對）	fǎnduì	v.	to oppose
任命	rènmìng	v.	to appoint ... as ...
辩论（辯論）	biànlùn	v./n.	to debate; debate
入党（黨）	rùdǎng	v.	to join a party

【练习】

一. 填空：

> 之所以...是因为...、高见、打破、以往、比方说、为了、
> 在...看来...、贿赂

台湾实行民主选举以来，大部分群众都积极投票。今年的投票率已经 ＿＿＿＿＿＿ 了以往的记录。现在的选民 ＿＿＿＿＿＿ 这么热情 ＿＿＿＿＿＿ 他们希望改变一些重要的基本国策。这自然是一件好事，但是民主选举也带来了很多不正之风。 ＿＿＿＿＿＿ ，有些候选人为了拉选票 ＿＿＿＿＿＿ 选民。 ＿＿＿＿＿＿ 那种挨家挨户访问的拉票方式已经不见了。民主选举还造成了其它一些问题，例如，有些家庭 ＿＿＿＿＿＿ 争论应该选谁常常吵架。有些人认为现在的民主选举并没有改变台湾的民主化。 ＿＿＿＿＿＿ 他们 ＿＿＿＿＿＿ ，投票率高只是社会动乱的征兆。你对这个问题有什么 ＿＿＿＿＿＿ ？

二. 完成句子(Complete the following sentences)：

1. 他以往上课总是无精打采，＿＿＿＿＿＿＿＿＿＿＿＿＿＿＿＿＿＿＿＿＿＿＿＿＿＿＿。

2. 毕业以后能不能找到好工作跟 ＿＿＿＿＿＿＿＿＿＿＿＿＿＿＿＿＿＿＿＿＿ 有关系？

3. 无论共和党还是民主党执政，＿＿＿＿＿＿＿＿＿＿＿＿＿＿＿＿＿＿＿＿＿＿＿＿＿。

4. 以现在的经济情况看来，＿＿＿＿＿＿＿＿＿＿＿＿＿＿＿＿＿＿＿＿＿＿＿＿＿＿＿。

5. 在竞选活动中那些候选人不是 ＿＿＿＿＿＿＿＿＿＿ 就是 ＿＿＿＿＿＿＿＿＿＿＿＿＿。

三. 用中文解释下列词组：

1. 杞人忧天

2. 无精打采

3. 宗教狂热

四. 造句：(Use more than one sentence for some of the phrases below in order to make the discourse function of the phrase clear.)

1. 在...情况下

2. 以往

3. 跟... 相去不远

4. 无论... 都

5. 到底

五. 作文：民主制度有哪些优点跟缺点？(The composition should consist of both general comments and specific statements. You should try to use as many linking words as possible)

【練習】

一. 填空：

> 之所以...是因為...、高見、打破、以往、比方説、為了、
> 在...看來...、賄賂

　　臺灣實行民主選舉以來，大部分羣眾都積極投票。今年的投票率已經
_____了以往的記錄。現在的選民_____這麼熱情_____他們希望
改　變一些重要的基本國策。這自然是一件好事，但是民主選舉也帶來了很
多不正之風。_____，有些候選人為了拉選票_____選民。_____那
種挨家挨戶訪問的拉票方式已經不見了。民主選舉還造成了其它一些問題，
例如，有些家庭_____爭論應該選誰常常吵架。有些人認為現在的民主選
舉並沒有改變臺灣的民主化。_____他們_____，投票率高只是社會動
亂的徵兆。你對這個問題有甚麼_____？

二. 完成句子(Complete the following sentences)：

1. 他以往上課總是無精打采，_____。

2. 畢業以後能不能找到好工作跟 _____ 有關係？

3. 無論共和黨還是民主黨執政，_____。

4. 以現在的經濟情況看來，_____。

5. 在競選活動中那些候選人不是 _____ 就是 _____。

三. 用中文解釋下列詞組：

1. 杞人憂天

2. 無精打采

3. 宗教狂熱

四. 造句： (Use more than one sentence for some of the phrases below in order to make the discourse function of the phrase clear.)

1. 在...情況下

2. 以往

3. 跟... 相去不遠

4. 無論... 都

5. 到底

五. 作文：民主制度有哪些優點跟缺點？ (The composition should consist of both general comments and specific statements. You should try to use as many linking words as possible.)

【衍生活动】

讨论与辩论：市长大选

　　我们想选出理想的市长，考虑了好久，还没办法决定。毕竟下面这三位候选人是各有所长，到底谁适合当市长？热心的朋友，用您的智慧，替我们拿个主意吧!

三位候选人简介：

1. <u>谦虚的政治学者</u>
　　　　性别：男
　　　　年龄：50
　　　　籍贯：北京
　　　　党籍：中国共产党
　　　　婚姻状况：已婚
　　　　学历：北京大学政治学博士
　　　　宗教：佛教
　　　　经历：曾任北京大学政治系教授、北京大学副校长
　　　　健康状况：有高血压
　　　　性格：温和、谦虚
　　　　做事态度：中庸之道
　　　　政见：以儒家思想为基础并有西方的民主精神
　　　　其他：不吸烟、不喝酒、素食主义者

2. <u>**热心的社会改革者**</u>

      性别：女

      年龄：46

      籍贯：台湾

      党籍：国民党

      婚姻状况：离婚

      学历：日本东京大学社会系毕业

      经历：妇女运动负责人，办过杂志、报纸

      健康状况：良好

      性格：独立、冷静、分析力强，会辩论

      做事态度：遇到问题有追根究底的精神

      政见：主张政治制度全盘西化、法律上人人平等，消除贫穷

      其他：相信男女平等，赞成同性恋合法

3. <u>**年轻的农业专家**</u>

      性别：男

      年龄：45

      籍贯：广东

      党籍：无

      婚姻状况：已婚

      学历：农业经济学博士

      经历：农业发展委员会主席、富裕县县长

      健康状况：一切正常

      性格：不自私、热情洋溢

      做事态度：敏感、小心、要求完美

      政见：尊重民意，注重社会和谐

      其他：房地产多，和工商业关系良好

【衍生活動】

討論與辯論：市長大選

　　我們想選出理想的市長，考慮了好久，還沒辦法決定。畢竟下面這三位候選人是各有所長，到底誰適合當市長？熱心的朋友，用您的智慧，替我們拿個主意吧！

三位候選人簡介：

1. <u>謙虛的政治學者</u>
　　　　性別：男
　　　　年齡：50
　　　　籍貫：北京
　　　　黨籍：中國共產黨
　　　　婚姻狀況：已婚
　　　　學歷：北京大學政治學博士
　　　　宗教：佛教
　　　　經歷：曾任北京大學政治系教授、北京大學副校長
　　　　健康狀況：有高血壓
　　　　性格：溫和、謙虛
　　　　做事態度：中庸之道
　　　　政見：以儒家思想為基礎並有西方的民主精神
　　　　其他：不吸煙、不喝酒、素食主義者

2. 熱心的社會改革者
　　　　　性別：女
　　　　　年齡：46
　　　　　籍貫：台灣
　　　　　黨籍：國民黨
　　　　　婚姻狀況：離婚
　　　　　學歷：日本東京大學社會系畢業
　　　　　經歷：婦女運動負責人，辦過雜誌、報紙
　　　　　健康狀況：良好
　　　　　性格：獨立、冷靜、分析力強，會辯論
　　　　　做事態度：遇到問題有追根究底的精神
　　　　　政見：主張政治制度全盤西化、法律上人人平等，消除貧窮
　　　　　其他：相信男女平等，贊成同性戀合法

3. 年輕的農業專家
　　　　　性別：男
　　　　　年齡：45
　　　　　籍貫：廣東
　　　　　黨籍：無
　　　　　婚姻狀況：已婚
　　　　　學歷：農業經濟學博士
　　　　　經歷：農業發展委員會主席、富裕縣縣長
　　　　　健康狀況：一切正常
　　　　　性格：不自私、熱情洋溢
　　　　　做事態度：敏感、小心、要求完美
　　　　　政見：尊重民意，注重社會和諧
　　　　　其他：房地產多，和工商業關係良好

【第十四課】

電影

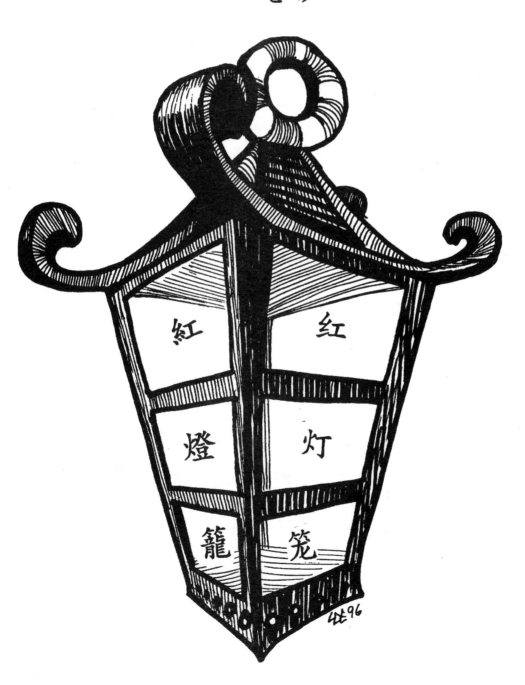

紅　紅
燈　灯
籠　笼

【课文】

讨论电影『大红灯笼高高挂』

陈先生： 听说你昨天租了『大红灯笼高高挂』录像带在家里看，有什么心得？是不是很庆幸自己活在二十世纪，不必受大男人主义者的压迫？

林小姐； 我不敢说二十世纪的女性完全不受男性的压迫，我只能说现在的情况比以前改善多了。这部片子整体看来，拍得真不错。制作严谨，导演手法成熟，镜头取得很美，再加上女主角的演技也到了炉火纯青的境界，这部电影真值得看。

陈先生： 可不是吗？我认为导演特别会营造气氛，虽然剧中包含了春、夏、秋、冬四个季节，不过为了配合剧情的需要，春、夏的喜悦与生命力就全都给藏了起来，取而代之的则是毫无生趣的黄昏、红灯笼和冬夜。除此之外，我认为每次"点灯"时的音效也做得相当成功。

林小姐： 您指的是一阵急促的锣鼓声吧？第一次鼓声配着红灯笼出场的时候，我觉得有一点突兀，慢慢地，就自然而然地把它们视为一体了。我猜导演一定学过心理学，他让人的视觉与听觉紧密地结合，随之也把观众的情绪带入高潮，安排得相当巧妙。另外，我也很欣赏饰演三姨太的那位女演员，她唱的几段京戏有板有眼，如果不是科班出身绝没有那种功力。

陈先生： 整部片子最让我纳闷的就是自始至终观众都没法儿看清楚老爷子的长相。不过在这部电影的原著「妻妾成群」小说中，作者对老爷子的长相则描写得清清楚楚。难道电影编剧想要暗示观众什么吗？

林小姐： 我想这部片子有很浓的反传统味道在内。整个陈家象征封建社会里的王室，妻妾像争宠的臣子，老爷子是影射君主。一方面君主高高在上，故做神秘，令人难以捉摸，另一方面君主也利用群臣之间的明争暗斗、争风吃醋巩固自己的地位。想想看，从古到今有多少平民百姓能见到君主呢？自然，观众就看不清老爷了。

陈先生： 提到明争暗斗、争风吃醋，记得有几幕戏是以姨太太彼此间的讥讽为主，不知你对女人那种"话中有话"、"话中带刺"、"骂人不带脏字儿"的对话方式有何高见？

林小姐： 您以为那种对话方式只有女人才会吗？那您真是太"小看"男人了。剧中的姨太太们之所以会说那种尖酸刻薄的话，都是因为长期受压迫，内心怨恨无处宣泄所造成的，追根究底罪魁祸首还是男人，不是吗？

陈先生： 我知道看完这部片子的女性对男性或多或少会有些不满。不管是封建时代的男女不平等，还是电影的故事情节，都跟现实社会不一样。我们大可不必为这些芝麻小事伤和气。过两天我请你去看『当莎丽遇上哈利』，算是向你赔不是，好吗？

林小姐： 算了，女人的悲哀你们男人是不会了解的。

【課文】

討論電影『大紅燈籠高高掛』

陳先生： 聽說你昨天租了『大紅燈籠高高掛』錄像帶在家裏看，有甚麼心得？是不是很慶幸自己活在二十世紀，不必受大男人主義者的壓迫？

林小姐： 我不敢說二十世紀的女性完全不受男性的壓迫，我只能說現在的情況比以前改善多了。這部片子整體看來，拍得真不錯。製作嚴謹，導演手法成熟，鏡頭取得很美，再加上女主角的演技也到了爐火純青的境界，這部電影真值得看。

陳先生： 可不是嗎？我認為導演特別會營造氣氛，雖然劇中包含了春、夏、秋、冬四個季節，不過為了配合劇情的需要，春、夏的喜悅與生命力就全都給藏了起來，取而代之的則是毫無生趣的黃昏、紅燈籠和冬夜。除此之外，我認為每次"點燈"時的音效也做得相當成功。

林小姐： 您指的是一陣急促的鑼鼓聲吧？第一次鼓聲配着紅燈籠出場的時候，我覺得有一點突兀，慢慢地，就自然而然地把它們視為一體了。我猜導演一定學過心理學，他讓人的視覺與聽覺緊密地結合，隨之也把觀眾的情緒帶入高潮，安排得相當巧妙。另外，我也很欣賞飾演三姨太的那位女演員，她唱的幾段京戲有板有眼，如果不是科班出身絕沒有那種功力。

陳先生： 整部片子最讓我納悶的就是自始至終觀眾都沒法兒看清楚老爺子的長相。不過在這部電影的原著『妻妾成羣』小說中，作者對老爺子的長相則描寫得清清楚楚。難道電影編劇想要暗示觀眾甚麼嗎？

林小姐： 我想這部片子有很濃的反傳統味道在內。整個陳家象徵封建社會裏的王室，妻妾像爭寵的臣子，老爺子是影射君主。一方面君主高高在上，故做神秘，令人難以捉摸，另一方面君主也利用羣臣之間的明爭暗斗、爭風吃醋鞏固自己的地位。想想看，從古到今有多少平民百姓能見到君主呢？自然，觀眾就看不清老爺了。

陳先生： 提到明爭暗鬥、爭風吃醋，記得有幾幕戲是以姨太太彼此間的譏諷為主，不知你對女人那種"話中有話"、"話中帶刺"、"罵人不帶髒字兒"的對話方式有何高見？

林小姐： 您以為那種對話方式只有女人才會嗎？那您真是太"小看"男人了。劇中的姨太太們之所以會說那種尖酸刻薄的話，都是因為長期受壓迫，內心怨恨無處宣泄所造成的，追根究底罪魁禍首還是男人，不是嗎？

陳先生： 我知道看完這部片子的女性對男性或多或少會有些不滿。不管是封建時代的男女不平等，還是電影的故事情節，都跟現實社會不一樣。我們大可不必為這些芝麻小事傷和氣。過兩天我請你去看『當莎麗遇上哈利』，算是向你賠不是，好嗎？

林小姐： 算了，女人的悲哀你們男人是不會了解的。

讨论题：

 1. 你用什么标准来决定一部电影的好坏？

 2. 请你介绍一部让你难忘的电影？

 3. 假如你是一个导演，你会拍什么主题的电影？为什么？

 3. 在『大红灯龙』这部电影中，你认为最值得讨论的问题是什么？

 5. 政府有没有权力禁演一部电影？为什么？

 6. 如果你有一个八岁的孩子，他在看电影的时候你会给他什么限制？

討論題：

 1. 你用甚麼標準來決定一部電影的好壞？

 2. 請你介紹一部讓你難忘的電影？

 3. 假如你是一個導演，你會拍甚麼主題的電影？為甚麼？

 3. 在《大紅燈龍》這部電影中，你認為最值得討論的問題是甚麼？

 5. 政府有沒有權力禁演一部電影？為甚麼？

 6. 如果你有一個八歲的孩子，他在看電影的時候你會給他甚麼限制？

【生词/生詞】

1. 灯笼（燈籠）	dēnglóng	n.	lantern
2. 租	zū	v.	to rent
3. 录像带（錄）	lùxiàngdài	n.	videotape
4. 心得	xīndé	n.	reflection
5. 庆幸（慶）	qìngxìng	v.	to rejoice
6. 压迫（壓）	yāpò	n./v.	oppression; to oppress
7. 改善	gǎishàn	v./n.	to improve; improvement
8. 拍	pāi	v.	to make (movies)
9. 严谨（嚴謹）	yánjǐn	adj.	(to be) rigorous, well-knit
10. 导演（導）	dǎoyǎn	n./v.	director (of movies); to direct
11. 成熟	chéngshú	adj.	(to be) mature
12. 镜头（鏡頭）	jìngtóu	n.	camera lens, shot
13. 演技	yǎnjì	n.	acting skill
14. 炉火纯青（爐、純）	lúhuǒchúnqīng	adv.p	highly professionalized
15. 境界	jìngjiè	n.	extent, boundary
16. 营造（營）	yíngzào	v.	to portray (in art/literature)
17. 气氛（氣）	qìfēn	n.	atmosphere
18. 包含	bāohán	v.	to contain
19. 配合	pèihé	v./n.	to cooperate; cooperation
20. 剧情（劇）	jùqíng	n.	plot (of a story)
21. 喜悦	xǐyuè	n.	happiness
22. 黄昏	huánghūn	n.	dusk
23. 音效	yīnxiào	n.	sound effects
24. 相当（當）	xiāngdāng	adj.	quite, reasonably
25. 锣鼓（鑼）	luógǔ	n.	gong and drum
26. 突兀	túwù	adj.	(to be) abrupt
27. 自然而然地	zìrán'érránde	adv.	naturally
28. 心理学（學）	xīnlǐxué	n.	psychology

29. 视觉（視覺）	shìjué	n.	sense of sight
30. 听觉（聽覺）	tīngjué	n.	sense of hearing
31. 紧密地（緊）	jǐnmìde	adv.	closely
32. 结合	jiéhé	v./n.	to integrate; integration
33. 安排	ānpái	v./n.	to arrange; arrangement
34. 巧妙	qiǎomiào	adj.	(to be) ingenious, clever
35. 饰演（飾）	shìyǎn	v.	to act as (in a performance)
36. 京戏（戲）	jīngxì	n.	Beijing opera
37. 有板有眼	yǒubǎnyǒuyǎn	adj.	(to be) rhythmical (in singing/speech)
38. 绝（絕）	jué	adv.	absolutely
39. 纳闷（納悶）	nàmèn	v.	to be confused, puzzled
40. 描写（寫）	miáoxiě	v.	to describe
41. 编剧（編劇）	biānjù	n.	playwright
42. 暗示	ànshì	v./n.	to give a hint; hint
43. 浓（濃）	nóng	adj.	(to be) strong, thick
44. 象征（徵）	xiàngzhēng	v./n.	to symbolize; symbol
45. 争宠（爭寵）	zhēngchǒng	v.	to struggle to be favored
46. 影射	yǐngshè	v.	to allude to
47. 故	gù	adv.	purposefully
48. 争风吃醋（爭風）	zhēngfēngchīcù	v.p.	to fight because of jealousy
49. 巩固（鞏）	gǒnggù	v.	to consolidate
50. 平民	píngmín	n.	common people
51. 提到	tídào	v.	to mention
52. 彼此	bǐcǐ	adv.	each other
53. 讽刺（諷）	fěngcì	v.	to satirize
54. 脏（臟）	zāng	adj.	(to be) dirty
55. 小看	xiǎokàn	v.	to look down
56. 尖酸刻薄	jiānsuānkèbó	v.p.	to be ruthless (in speaking)
57. 怨恨	yuànhèn	n.	resentment and hatred
58. 宣泄	xuānxiè	v./n.	to release; resentment
59. 追根究底	zhuīgēnjiūdǐ	v.p.	to probe into (something)

60. 罪魁祸首〔禍〕	zuìkuíhuòshǒu	n.	chief criminal
61. 或多或少	huòduōhuòshǎo	adv.	more or less
62. 悲哀	bēi'āi	n./v.	grief; to be grieved

【句型】

一. 整体看来/整體看來 *adverbial phrase*: overall, to look at it as a whole

  1. 整体看来这部电影有很浓的反传统味道。

    （整體看來這部電影有很濃的反傳統味道。）

    "On the whole, this film is strongly against tradition."

  2. 他导演的电影，整体看来都很严谨，可是有的情节也很离奇。

    （他導演的電影，整體看來都很嚴謹，可是有的情節也很離奇。）

    "The movies he directed are very well-knit in general, but some plots are very bizarre."

二. 值得/值得 *verb phrase*: to be worth (doing), worthwhile

  1. 这个故事情节感人肺腑，值得读。

    （這個故事情節感人肺腑，值得讀。）

    "This story really touches peoples' hearts, so it is worth reading."

  2. 为了事业牺牲家庭值得吗？

    （為了事業犧牲家庭值得嗎？）

    "Is it worthwhile to sacrifice one's family for one's career?"

三. 毫无/毫無 *adverbial phrase*: without any... (There are many commonly used phrases of this kind: 毫无意义/毫無意義，毫无道理/毫無道理，毫无印象/毫無印象，毫无兴趣/毫無興趣，毫无理由/毫無理由)

  1. 我对恐怖电影毫无兴趣。

    （我對恐怖電影毫無興趣。）

    "I am not interested in horror movies at all."

2. 他说多子多福的传统观念毫无道理。

（他說多子多福的傳統觀念毫無道理。）

"He says that the traditional concept of 'the more children, the better' does not make any sense."

四. 自始至终/自始至終 *adverbial phrase*: from beginning to end

1. 自始至终观众都没有看清楚男主角的长相。

（自始至終觀眾都沒有看清楚男主角的長相。）

"From beginning to end, the audience has no way of seeing a clear picture of the leading male actor."

2. 那部电影的剧情自始至终都让人觉得很沉闷。

（那部電影的劇情自始至終都讓人覺得很沉悶。）

"The film's story makes people feel depressed from the beginning to the end."

五. 以...为主/以...為主 *verb phrase*: to regard/treat ... as the primary...

1. 鲁迅的散文是不是以讥讽为主？

（魯迅的散文是不是以譏諷為主？）

"Is it true that Lu Xun's short essays are primarily ironic?"

2. 中国北方人的饮食以蔬菜和面食为主。

（中國北方人的飲食以蔬菜和面食為主。）

"The diet of the northerners in China is chiefly vegetables and flour-based foods."

六. 对...有何高见/對...有何高見 *verb phrase*: What is your viewpoint on ...; This is a more formal way of saying 对...有什么看法/對...有甚麼看法。

1. 你对如何解决贩毒的问题有何高见？

（你對如何解決販毒的問題有何高見？）

"What is your view on how to solve the problem of drug dealing?"

2. 你对如何学好中文有何高见？

（你對如何學好中文有何高見？）

"How do you think we can learn Chinese well?"

七. 对…不满/對…不滿 *verb phrase*: dislike…, not satisfied with…; The positive sentence of this pattern is 对…满意/對…滿意。

1. 由于他一再失恋，他现在好像对所有的女性都有些不满。
   （由於他一再失戀，他現在好像對所有的女性都有些不滿。）

   "Because he has been disappointed in his love affairs over and over again, he seems to dislike all women now."

2. 在你看过的中国电影里你对哪位导演最满意？
   （在你看過的中國電影裏你對哪位導演最滿意？）

   "Among the Chinese movies you have seen, whose directing did you like best?"

八. 为…伤和气/為…傷和氣 *verb phrase*: to become angry with one another because (of)…

1. 为一些芝麻小事伤和气值得吗？
   （為一些芝麻小事傷和氣值得嗎？）

   "Is it worthwhile to become angry with each other because of trivial matters?"

2. 为政见不同跟朋友伤和气的事常常发生吗？
   （為政見不同跟朋友傷和氣的事常常發生嗎？）

   "Is it common for friends to become angry with each other because of different political viewpoints?"

九. 向…赔不是/向…賠不是 *verb phrase*: say sorry to …, apologize to …

1. 你会向你的朋友赔不是吗？
   （你會向你的朋友賠不是嗎？）

   "Can you tell your friends you are sorry?"

2. 有些人知道自己错了也不向别人陪不是。这是为什么？
   （有些人知道自己錯了也不向別人陪不是。這是為甚麼？）

   "Some people do not apologize to other people even though they know they are wrong themselves. Why is this?

【语法/語法】

"把"字句
(Bǎ Constructions)

In Lesson Two, we discussed word order in Chinese and mentioned that Chinese has SVO as its basic word order. In this lesson, we will focus on one of the alternative word orders, that is, 把字句 (the bǎ construction), and show how students can distinguish this construction from the basic word order. The structure of the bǎ construction is: subject-bǎ-object-verb, as shown in the following sentences:

1. 他把我的书放在桌子上。/他把我的書放在桌子上。

   "He put my book on the table."

2. 我还沒把作业作完。/我還沒把作業作完。

   "I have not finished my homework."

3. 学生把他看成他们的楷模。/學生把他看成他們的楷模。

   "Students treat him as their model."

There are a number of reasons for using the bǎ construction. Syntactically, all three of the sentences above must use the bǎ construction since the regular word order (i.e. SVO) cannot be used because of the postverb complements--在桌子上、完、他们的楷模。 Furthermore, all of these complements are necessary because without them the verbs in the sentences are left monosyllabic, which is not allowed in the bǎ construction.

Semantically, the bǎ construction differs from the SVO construction in that the verb in the bǎ construction cannot be possessive, whereas those in the SVO construction can be. For instance:

4. * 我现在把那两本书有了。/我現在把那兩本書有了。

5. 我现在有了那两本书。/我現在有了那兩本書。

   "Now I have those two books."

有 is a possessive verb, and it is not acceptable in the bǎ construction as shown in 4; however, it is acceptable in sentence 5. Another semantic feature of the verb in the bǎ construction is that it is likely to be affective. That is, the action of the verb often affects the object in the sentence. An example of this is given in sentence 6.

6. 我的朋友常把我的屋子弄乱。/我的朋友常把我的屋子弄亂。
   "My friends often mess up my room."
7. *我把我朋友喜欢。/我把我朋友喜歡。
8. 我喜欢我的朋友。/我喜歡我的朋友。
   "I like my friends."

Both sentences 6 and 7 are bǎ constructions, yet one has an affective verb and the other does not, which consequently conditions the grammaticality of the two sentences. However, from sentence 8 we see that this condition does not apply to the SVO construction. Another aspect that should be taken into consideration in differentiating the bǎ construction from the SVO construction is discourse-pragmatics. Many studies show that the object of the bǎ construction is almost always definite (i.e. mentioned in the previous discourse or known to both speaker(s) and listener(s) based on common knowledge). But this is not the case for the object in the SVO construction, as shown below:

9. *他把一本书看了。/他把一本書看了。
10. 他看了一本书。/他看了一本書。 "I have read a book."

Furthermore, if both the bǎ construction and the SVO construction are possible in a given discourse, the choice of one construction over the other often depends upon the importance of the object: the object in the bǎ construction is more important than that in the SVO construction.

We have seen that the use of the bǎ construction and the SVO construction can be conditioned by syntactic, semantic, and discourse-pragmatic factors. All of these factors are equally important for students, especially advanced students, to learn.

【补充词汇/補充詞彙】

侦探片 （偵）	zhēntànpiàn	n.	detective film
恐怖片	kǒngbùpiàn	n.	horror film
科幻片	kēhuànpiàn	n.	science fiction film
文艺片 （藝）	wényìpiàn	n.	literary/art film
色情片	sèqíngpiàn	n.	X-rated film
主角	zhǔjué	n.	leading actor/actress
配角	pèijué	n.	supporting actor/actress
明星	míngxīng	n.	(movie) star
演员 （員）	yǎnyuán	n.	actor/actress
影迷	yǐngmí	n.	movie fan
编剧 （編劇）	biānjù	n.	scriptwriter
悲剧 （劇）	bēijù	n.	tragedy
喜剧 （劇）	xǐjù	n.	comedy
改编 （編）	gǎibiān	v.	to adapt, to revise
原著	yuánzhù	n.	author of original work
剧情 （劇）	jùqíng	n.	story
情节 （節）	qíngjié	n.	plot
影评 （評）	yǐngpíng	n.	film critique
配音	pèiyīn	v.	to dub
旁白	pángbái	n.	narration
布景	bùjǐng	n.	setting, backdrop
灯光 （燈）	dēngguāng	n.	lighting
音效	yīnxiào	n.	sound effect
剪接	jiǎnjiē	v.	to edit
字幕	zìmù	n.	subtitle
感人	gǎnrén	v.p.	to be moving
曲折	qūzhé	adj.	(to be) complicated
离奇 （離）	líqí	adj.	(to be) bizarre

【练习】

一. 填空：

　　　　以...为主，记录，对...不满，虽然，值得，自始至终，
　　　　之所以...是因为...

　　　张艺谋是中国第五代导演中最出色的一位。他导演的电影大部分都很
_____ 看。他导演的很多电影都_____描写女性 _____，在我看来，
最成功的一部是『菊豆』(Judou)。这部电影有很浓的反传统的味道。
_____ 中国政府很多人 _____ 这部电影的政治暗示 _____，海外很
多观众却很欣赏。一九九一年『菊豆』在美国打破了中文电影的卖座 _____。
有人认为，这部电影 _____那么成功 _____导演找到了一个演技完美的
女主角。从一九八八年拍『红高粱』到一九九五年拍『摇啊摇，摇到外婆
桥』，张艺谋跟女影星巩俐 _____ 都合作得很好。

二. 用所给词语改写下列句子：

1. 十年以前他看过那个电影，可是他现在已经忘了那个电影的剧情。〔毫无印象〕

2. 这部电影跟原著差了十万八千里，很多观众都不喜欢改编的剧情。〔对...不满〕

3. 他写的文学作品差不多都是小说。〔以...为主〕

4. 有人说："音乐没有国界，即使语言不同的人也可以通过音乐进行交流。" 你觉得这种说法有道理吗？（对...有何高见）

5. 春天跟夏天的喜悦全被导演藏了起来。（把...）

三. 造句: In order to use the phrases below, you need to write short paragraphs, not just individual sentences.

1. 我不敢说..., 只能说... (to express one's opinion)

2. 可不是吗? (to express agreement)

3. 自始至终

4. 整体看来..., 再加上...

四. 用中文解释下列词语的意思:

1. 高潮迭起

2. 难得一见

3. 尖酸刻薄

五. 谈谈你最喜欢的一部电影。(It should include a summary of the movie and your own reflection. Try to use as many bǎ constructions as possible.)

【練習】

一. 填空：

> 以…為主，記錄，對…不滿，雖然，值得，自始至終，
> 之所以…是因為…

　　張藝謀是中國第五代導演中最出色的一位。他導演的電影大部分都很 ＿＿＿＿＿＿ 看。他導演的很多電影都 ＿＿＿＿＿＿ 描寫女性 ＿＿＿＿＿＿ ，在我看來，最成功的一部是『菊豆』(Judou)。這部電影有很濃的反傳統的味道。＿＿＿＿＿＿ 中國政府很多人 ＿＿＿＿＿＿ 這部電影的政治暗示 ＿＿＿＿＿＿ ，海外很多觀眾卻很欣賞。一九九一年『菊豆』在美國打破了中文電影的賣座 ＿＿＿＿＿＿ 。有人認為，這部電影 ＿＿＿＿＿＿ 那麼成功 ＿＿＿＿＿＿ 導演找到了一個演技完美的女主角。從一九八八年拍『紅高粱』到一九九五年拍『搖啊搖，搖到外婆橋』，張藝謀跟女影星鞏俐 ＿＿＿＿＿＿ 都合作得很好。

二. 用所給詞語改寫下列句子：

1. 十年以前他看過那個電影，可是他現在已經忘了那個電影的劇情。（毫無印象）

2. 這部電影跟原著差了十萬八千里，很多觀眾都不喜歡改編的劇情。（對…不滿）

3. 他寫的文學作品差不多都是小說。（以…為主）

4. 有人說："音樂沒有國界，即使語言不同人們也可以通過音樂進行交流。"你覺得這種說法有道理嗎？ （對...有何高見）

5. 春天跟夏天的喜悦全被導演藏了起來。 （把...）

三. 造句: In order to use the phrases below, you need to write short paragraphs, not just individual sentences.

1. 我不敢說..., 只能說... (to express one's opinion)

2. 可不是嗎? (to express agreement)

3. 自始至終

4. 整體看來..., 再加上...

四. 用中文解釋下列詞語的意思:

1. 高潮迭起

2. 難得一見

3. 尖酸刻薄

五. 談談你最喜歡的一部電影。(It should include a summary of the movie and your own reflection. Try to use as many bǎ constructions as possible.)

【衍生活动】

解决问题：陈伟的难题

陈伟热爱电影艺术，下学期他打算选一门电影课。不过，教授很厉害，给了学生五个电影的难题。如果陈伟不能在两天之内回答这些问题，他就没有资格选这门课。好心的同学，请你们在课堂上讨论，替他找出答案。

1. 拍电影需要哪些工作人员？他们的责任是什么？
2. 看电影跟看小说有什么不同？
3. 如果一部电影没有高潮能不能算是好电影？
4. 为什么西方很多著名的戏剧是悲剧？
5. 拍电影应不应该考虑到社会责任，为什么？

【衍生活動】

解決問題：陳偉的難題

陳偉熱愛電影藝術，下學期他打算選一門電影課。不過，教授很厲害，給了學生五個電影的難題。如果陳偉不能在兩天之內回答這些問題，他就沒有資格選這門課。好心的同學，請你們在課堂上討論，替他找出答案。

1. 拍電影需要哪些工作人員？他們的責任是甚麼？
2. 看電影跟看小說有甚麼不同？
3. 如果一部電影沒有高潮能不能算是好電影？
4. 爲甚麼西方很多著名的戲劇是悲劇？
5. 拍電影應不應該考慮到社會責任？爲甚麼？

【第十五课】

即席讲演

即席演讲参考题目：

1. 谈谈你对离婚的看法。
2. 毒品合法，对现在的毒品问题有什么影响？
3. 我对男女平等的看法。
4. 人在痛苦的时候，常用哪些法子解决？
5. 我为什么要念大学？
6. 我最喜欢的一部电影。
7. 如何解决美国流浪汉的问题？
8. 一次难忘的约会（或聚会）。
9. 我学中文的感受。
10. 我的童年。
11. 我最尊敬的人。
12. 我心目中的中国。
13. 为什么一个国家要有国歌？
14. 我对爱情的看法。
15. 民主制度有哪些优点和缺点？

【第十五課】

即席講演

即席演講參考題目：

1. 談談你對離婚的看法。
2. 毒品合法，對現在的毒品問題有甚麼影響？
3. 我對男女平等的看法。
4. 人在痛苦的時候，常用哪些法子解決？
5. 我為甚麼要念大學？
6. 我最喜歡的一部電影。
7. 如何解決美國流浪漢的問題？
8. 一次難忘的約會（或聚會）。
9. 我學中文的感受。
10. 我的童年。
11. 我最尊敬的人。
12. 我心目中的中國。
13. 為甚麼一個國家要有國歌？
14. 我對愛情的看法。
15. 民主制度有哪些優點和缺點？

【练习】

仿照所给的例句造句：

一生的经验

从小我就是一个认真过日子的人，五岁那年我开始写日记，这个习惯一直维持了八十多年，现在看过去的日记是我一生中最大的乐趣。在里面我看到了自己成长的过程。现在也请你谈谈你的人生经验和对未来的认识，别忘了用四字成语：

五岁那一年，我明白父母并不喜欢追根究底的孩子。
五岁那一年，我明白…

八岁那一年，我认为巧克力、蛋糕是我百吃不厌的东西。
八岁那一年，我认为…

十岁那一年，我知道把吃完的口香糖丢在地上，是自私自利的行为。
十岁那一年，我知道…

十六岁那一年，我了解油腔滑调的男孩并不能吸引漂亮女孩的注意。
十六岁那一年，我了解…

二十一岁那一年，我发现爱情会使我的功课一落千丈。
二十一岁那一年，我发现…

二十八歲那一年，我明白跟父母聊天的時候千萬不要談到傳宗接代的話題。
二十八歲那一年，我明白...

三十三歲那一年，我了解直言不諱常讓我丟掉工作。
三十三歲那一年，我才能了解...

四十歲那一年，我明白隨心所欲總會得到惡果。
四十歲那一年，我才能明白...

四十九歲那一年，我才知道自始至終我都不瞭解我的太太。
四十九歲那一年，我才會知道...

五十五歲那一年，我才真的知道戒酒戒煙都是知易行難的事。
五十五歲那一年，我才能真的知道...

六十歲那一年，我了解衣錦還鄉只是為了面子。
六十歲那一年，我才會了解...

七十歲那一年，我想通了，只有出家才能讓人徹底脫離苦海。
七十歲那一年，我才會...

八十一歲那一年，我真的知道時間是千金難買的東西。
八十一歲那一年，我才能真的知道...

【練習】

做照所給的例句造句：

一生的經驗

　　從小我就是一個認真過日子的人，五歲那年我開始寫日記，這個習慣一直維持了八十多年，現在看過去的日記是我一生中最大的樂趣。在裡面我看到了自己成長的過程。現在也請你談談你的人生經驗和對未來的認識，別忘了用四字成語：

五歲那一年，我明白父母並不喜歡追根究底的孩子。
五歲那一年，我明白...

八歲那一年，我認為巧克力、蛋糕是我百吃不厭的東西。
八歲那一年，我認為...

十歲那一年，我知道把吃完的口香糖丟在地上，是自私自利的行為。
十歲那一年，我知道...

十六歲那一年，我了解油腔滑調的男孩並不能吸引漂亮女孩的注意。
十六歲那一年，我了解...

二十一歲那一年，我發現愛情會使我的功課一落千丈。
二十一歲那一年，我發現...

二十八岁那一年，我明白跟父母聊天的时候千万不要谈到传宗接代的话题。
二十八岁那一年，我会明白…

三十三岁那一年，我了解直言不讳常让我丢掉工作。
三十三岁那一年，我才会了解…

四十岁那一年，我明白随心所欲总会得到恶果。
四十岁那一年，我才能明白…

四十九岁那一年，我才知道自始至终我都不了解我的太太。
四十九岁那一年，我才会知道…

五十五岁那一年，我才真的知道戒酒戒烟都是知易行难的事。
五十五岁那一年，我才能真的知道…

六十岁那一年，我了解衣锦还乡只是为了面子。
六十岁那一年，我才会了解…

七十岁那一年，我想通了，只有出家才能让人彻底脱离苦海。
七十岁那一年，我才会…

八十一岁那一年，我真的知道时间是千金难买的东西。
八十一岁那一年，我才能真的知道…

【生词索引】
Vocabulary Index

Character 汉字	Pinyin 拼音	English Gloss 英译	Lesson # 课号
爱情	àiqíng	love	(9)
爱上了	àishàngle	to fall in love with	(12)
安静	ānjìng	(to be) quiet	(12)
案例	ànlì	precedent (of criminal investigation)	(8)
安排	ānpái	to arrange; arrangement	(14)
暗示	ànshì	to give a hint; hint	(14)
熬出头	áochūtóu	to bring an end to	(10)
安稳	ānwěn	to be smooth and steady	(13)
白	bái	for nothing, in vain	(5)
百吃不厌	bǎichībúyàn	to never get tired of eating	(6)
白老鼠	báilǎoshǔ	guinea pig	(8)
摆脱	bǎituō	to get rid of	(12)
报道	bàodào	to report; report	(13)
包含	bāohán	to contain	(14)
暴力	bàolì	violence	(13)
包容	bāoróng	to forgive	(9)
报应	bàoyìng	retribution	(10)
悲哀	bēi'āi	grief; to be grieved	(14)
被告	bèigào	defendant	(8)
背景	bèijǐng	background	(1)
悲伤	bēishāng	grief; to be grieved	(10)
本来	běnlái	originally	(10)
编剧	biānjù	playwright	(14)

辨识	biànshí	to distinguish	(8)
标准	biāozhǔn	standard	(12)
彼此	bǐcǐ	each other	(9)&(14)
毕竟	bìjìng	after all	(9)
必须	bìxū	must	(11)
必需品	bìxūpǐn	product of daily needs	(11)
必要	bìyào	(to be) necessary	(5)
比喻	bǐyù	metaphor	(11)
博士	bóshì	doctor (degree)	(11)
补充	bǔchōng	to supplement; supplement	(6)
不到	búdào	to be less than	(3)
不过	búguò	however	(13)
不仅如此	bùjǐnrúcǐ	not only that	(3)
不耐烦	búnàifán	to be impatient	(3)
不人道	bùréndào	inhumane	(8)
不幸	búxìng	to be unfortunate	(10)
猜出	cāichū	to guess	(1)
采用	cǎiyòng	to adopt	(11)
参加	cānjiā	to participate in, to join	(3)
餐厅	cāntīng	dining hall	(5)
查	chá	to check, to examine	(8)
柴可夫斯基	cháikěfūsījī	Tchaikovsky	(7)
搀	chān	to mix	(8)
产品	chǎnpǐn	product	(3)
产生	chǎnshēng	to produce, to come into being	(13)
尝	cháng	to taste	(5)
吵架	chǎojià	to quarrel; quarrel	(13)
潮流	cháolíu	tide	(11)
超越	chāoyuè	to surpass	(7)
撤消	chèxiāo	to dismiss, to revoke	(2)
车站	chēzhàn	(bus)stop, (train)terminal	(10)
趁早	chènzǎo	before it is too late	(10)

点	diǎn	to order (dishes)	(5)
典礼	diǎnlǐ	ceremony	(12)
抵抗	dǐkàng	to resist	(9)
地位	dìwèi	status	(12)
地铁	dìxiàtiě	subway	(10)
凋零	diāolíng	to wither	(11)
定义	dìngyì	definition	(9)
动机	dòngjī	motivation	(13)
动乱	dòngluàn	disturbance, turmoil	(13)
豆沙	dòushā	bean paste	(6)
豆芽	dòuyá	bean sprout	(6)
毒	dú	(to be) merciless	(2)
独裁者	dúcáizhě	dictator	(2)
毒贩	dúfàn	drug dealer	(8)
独立	dúlì	(to be) independent; independence	(12)
毒品	dúpǐn	drugs	(8)
毒药	dúyào	poison	(10)
毒瘾	dúyǐn	drug addiction	(8)
对劲	duìjìn	(to feel) right (colloq.)	(5)
恶	è	evil intention; (to be) evil	(9)
饿死	èsǐ	to starve to death	(11)
恩慈	ēncí	kindness	(9)
发表	fābiǎo	to publish (articles)	(4)
发怒	fānù	to become angry	(9)
法师	fǎshī	(title) Buddhist priest	(9)
法庭	fǎtíng	court	(8)
发作	fāzuò	(of addiction, disease) to start	(8)
反	fǎn	to oppose	(13)
烦恼	fánnǎo	agitation; (to be) agitated	(7)
犯法	fànfǎ	to commit a crime	(8)
凡人	fánrén	ordinary human being	(9)
反映	fǎnyìng	to reflect	(7)

翻阅	fānyuè	to browse, to read	(9)
烦躁不安	fánzàobù'ān	to be annoyed	(7)
反正	fǎnzhèng	in any case, anyway	(5)
方便	fāngbiàn	to be convenient; convenience	(3)
放弃	fàngqì	to abandon	(10)
方式	fāngshì	style	(13)
费用	fèiyòng	expense	(8)
粉笔	fěnbǐ	chalk	(4)
分化	fēnhuà	to split up	(13)
愤怒	fènnù	indignation; to be angry	(10)
讽刺	fěngcì	to satirize	(14)
风格	fēnggé	style	(7)
风气	fēngqì	atmosphere	(11)
佛教	fójiào	Buddhism	(11)
否定	fǒudìng	to deny	(11)
否则	fǒuzé	otherwise	(10)
福利	fúlì	benefit	(10)
付钱	fùqián	to pay	(5)
服务	fúwù	service	(8)
富裕	fùyù	(to be) wealthy	(10)
改善	gǎishàn	to improve; improvement	(14)
干脆	gāncuì	straightforwardly; (to be) straightforward	(3)
甘心	gānxīn	to be willing	(10)
刚	gāng	just	(1)
钢琴曲	gāngqínqǔ	piano concerto	(7)
搞	gǎo	to do (e.g. research)	(4)
高考	gāokǎo	college entrance exam	(5)
高手	gāoshǒu	master	(3)
高雅	gāoyǎ	(to be) noble and elegant	(7)
高枕无忧	gāozhěnwúyōu	to be worry-free	(10)
各行各业	gèhánggèyè	every field of work	(4)
哥林多前书	gēlínduōqiánshū	1 Corinthians	(9)

根	gēn	root	(11)
根基	gēnjī	foundation	(11)
根据	gēnjù	according to; grounds	(2)
公布	gōngbù	to announce	(13)
巩固	gǒnggù	to consolidate	(14)
公平	gōngpíng	(to be) fair	(8)
故	gù	purposefully	(14)
辜负	gūfù	to let down	(11)
古典	gǔdiǎn	(to be) classical	(7)
顾客	gùkè	customer	(3)
鼓励	gǔlì	to encourage; encouragement	(13)
固执	gùzhí	(to be) stubborn	(5)
挂	guà	to hang	(3)
怪味（儿）	guàiwèi(er)	strange taste or smell	(5)
观众	guānzhòng	audience	(14)
光	guāng	only	(11)
广告	guǎnggào	advertisement	(3)
过程	guòchéng	process	(8)
过期	guòqī	to pass the expiration date; to be overdue	(5)
海鲜	hǎixiān	seafood	(6)
害羞	hàixiū	to be shy, bashful	(9)
含笑而过	hánxiào'érguò	to pass with a smile	(9)
寒喧	hánxuān	to chat	(13)
好象	hǎoxiàng	to seem, to appear	(1)
恒久	héngjīu	everlasting	(9)
红烧鱼	hóngshāoyú	braised fish with soy sauce	(6)
候选人	hòuxuǎnrén	candidate	(13)
怀孕	huáiyùn	to be pregnant	(9)
环保	huánbǎo	environmental protection	(13)
黄昏	huánghūn	dusk	(14)
黄金	huángjīn	(yellow) gold	(12)
谎言	huǎngyán	lie	(3)

灰	huī	dust, ash	(4)
贿赂	huìlù	to bribe	(13)
回忆	huíyì	to recollect; recall	(1)
浑然忘我	húnránwàngwǒ	to be totally involved	(7)
活动	huódòng	activity	(13)
或多或少	huòduōhuòshǎo	more or less	(14)
活力	huólì	vitality	(7)
忌	jì	to restrain from	(6)
基础	jīchǔ	basis, foundation	(10)
缉毒	jìdú	to apprehend drug dealers	(8)
忌妒	jìdù	to be jealous	(9)
讥讽	jīfěng	to mock	(14)
几乎	jīhū	almost	(13)
计划	jìhuà	to plan; plan	(6)
积极	jījí	(to be) active	(13)
计较	jìjiào	to fuss about	(9)
技能	jìnéng	skill	(10)
寂寞无聊	jìmòwúliáo	to be lonely and bored	(9)
寄托	jìtuō	placing (e.g. hope) on; to place (e.g. hope) on	(7)
积蓄	jīxù	savings; to save (money)	(10)
价格	jiàgé	price	(3)
家教	jiājiào	private tutor	(5)
假如	jiǎrú	if...	(1)
家庭	jiātíng	family	(1)
加薪	jiāxīn	to raise someone's salary	(6)
价值	jiàzhí	significance, value	(9)
价值观	jiàzhíguān	outlook, value concept	(12)
检举	jiǎnjǔ	to report (a legal offender)	(8)
建立	jiànlì	to establish	(11)
尖酸刻薄	jiānsuānkèbó	to be ruthless (in speaking)	(14)
见外	jiànwài	to regard oneself as an outsider	(6)

简直	jiǎnzhí	simply, extremely	(10)
讲理	jiǎnglǐ	to reason	(5)
奖券	jiǎngquàn	bonus certificate	(3)
浇	jiāo	to pour liquid on	(10)
交代	jiāodài	to explain (unwillingly)	(8)
角度	jiǎodù	angle, perspective	(12)
教诲	jiàohuì	teaching, instruction	(11)
交响曲	jiāoxiǎngqǔ	symphony	(7)
教育	jiàoyù	to educate; education	(1)
戒	jiè	to give up (e.g. drinking)	(10)
解除	jiěchú	to remove	(7)
解雇	jiěgù	to fire, to dismiss	(4)
结果	jiéguǒ	result	(13)
结合	jiéhé	to integrate; integration	(14)
结论	jiélùn	conclusion	(13)
近乎	jìnhū	almost	(10)
津津有味	jīnjīnyǒuwèi	with great pleasure	(12)
紧密地	jǐnmìde	closely	(14)
警官	jǐngguān	police officer	(8)
警界	jǐngjiè	the police profession	(8)
境界	jìngjiè	extent, boundary	(14)
敬佩	jìngpèi	to respect, to admire	(2)
景气	jǐngqì	(to be) prosperous	(8)
警犬	jǐngquǎn	police dog	(8)
镜头	jìngtóu	camera lens, shot	(14)
京戏	jīngxì	Beijing opera	(14)
竞选	jìngxuǎn	to run for office	(13)
精致	jīngzhì	(to be) elegant	(6)
举	jǔ	to give (an example)	(2)
举办	jǔbàn	to hold (e.g. meetings)	(13)
剧情	jùqíng	plot (of a story)	(14)
眷属	juànshǔ	family members	(12)

决	jué	absolutely	(14)
觉得	juéde	to feel	(2)
爵士乐	juéshìyuè	jazz	(7)
开创	kāichuàng	to start, to initiate	(11)
刊登	kāndēng	to publish (e.g. newspapers)	(13)
可惜	kěxī	to pity	(10)
科研	kēyán	scientific research	(4)
恐怕	kǒngpà	to be afraid of	(6)
苦衷	kǔzhōng	something difficult to discuss	(2)
夸耀	kuāyào	to praise	(12)
快乐	kuàilè	(to be) happy; happiness	(12)
困绕	kùnrǎo	to be puzzled	(9)
垃圾	lājī	garbage	(11)
拉票	lāpiào	to solicit votes	(13)
来之不易	láizhībúyì	not easy to obtain	(4)
狼狈	lángbèi	(to be) awkward	(10)
浪费	làngfèi	to waste	(11)
浪漫	làngmàn	(to be) romantic	(7)
老	lǎo	often	(6)
老实说	lǎoshíshuō	honestly speaking	(8)
老外	lǎowài	foreigner (colloq.)	(5)
勒索	lèsuǒ	to blackmail	(8)
类似	lèisì	(to be) similar	(8)
冷静	lěngjìng	(to be) calm	(2)
立	lì	to erect (a sign)	(9)
理论	lǐlùn	to reason; theory	(5)
理想	lǐxiǎng	ideal	(13)
理性	lǐxìng	ration	(13)
利益	lìyì	benefit	(2)
理由	lǐyóu	reason	(11)
理智	lǐzhì	reason, intellect; (to be) reasonable	(7)
例子	lìzi	example	(2)

良知	liángzhī	conscience	(11)
了不起	liǎobùqǐ	to be extraordinary	(2)
了解	liǎojiě	to understand; understanding	(1)
临	lín	right before	(10)
零工	línggōng	part-time job	(10)
灵敏	língmǐn	(to be) sensitive	(8)
领悟	lǐngwù	to understand	(9)
流浪汉	líulànghàn	homeless man	(10)
流行	líuxíng	(to be) popular	(7)
率	lǜ	ratio	(13)
炉火纯青	lúhuǒchúnqīng	highly professionalized	(14)
律师	lǜshī	lawyer	(4)
录像带	lùxiàngdài	videotape	(14)
沦落	lúnluò	to fall low	(10)
论文	lùnwén	research paper, dissertation, thesis (4)&(11)	
锣鼓	luógǔ	gong and drum	(14)
落伍	luòwǔ	to fall behind	(13)
麻婆豆腐	mápódòufutofu	cooked with peppercorns	(5)
卖春	màichūn	to be a prostitute	(8)
瞒不住	mánbúzhù	cannot hide	(9)
漫长	màncháng	long, endless	(10)
慢慢地	mànmànde	slowly	(1)
埋怨	mányuàn	blame; to blame	(10)
媒体	méitǐ	media	(13)
面对	miànduì	to face	(8)
免费	miǎnfèi	free of charge	(3)
勉强	miǎnqiǎng	to force one to do; (to be) reluctant	(11)
绵延不绝	miányánbùjué	to be everlasting	(9)
描述	miáoshù	to describe; description	(2)
描写	miáoxiě	to describe	(14)
民生	mínshēng	people's livelihood	(11)
民乐	mínyuè	folk music	(7)

认真	rènzhēn	to be serious, diligent	(1)
仍然	réngrán	still	(10)
日以继夜	rìyǐjìyè	day and night	(10)
儒家	rújiā	the Confucianists	(11)
洒脱	sǎtuō	to be free and easy in style	(7)
丧命	sàngmìng	to lose one's life	(8)
丧失	sàngshī	to lose	(13)
沙锅	shāguō	earthenware pot	(6)
煽动	shāndòng	to instigate	(13)
伤害	shānghài	to hurt	(5)
上进	shàngjìn	to strive to make progress	(10)
上诉	shàngsù	to appeal (legal term)	(8)
伤透	shāngtòu	to be bothersome	(8)
商业	shāngyè	commerce	(3)
深渊	shēnyuān	abyss	(9)
甚至	shènzhì	even	(10)
圣经	shèngjīng	Bible	(9)
生鱼片	shēngyúpiàn	raw sliced fish	(6)
失败	shībài	failure; to be defeated	(10)
市场	shìchǎng	market	(11)
时代	shídài	time, age, era	(11)
食古不化	shígǔbúhuà	(to be) pedantic	(11)
实际	shíjì	reality, fact; in fact	(1))
实际上	shíjìshàng	in fact	(4)
事件	shìjiàn	event, incident	(2)
视觉	shìjué	sense of sight	(14)
失去	shīqù	to lose	(7)
事实	shìshí	fact	(4)
食随知味	shísuízhīwèi	to experience and savor	(9)
史特劳斯	shǐtèláosī	Strauss	(7)
实行	shíxíng	to carry out (policy)	(13)
实验	shíyàn	to experiment	(8)

饰演	shìyǎn	to act as (in a performance)	(14)
受	shòu	passive marker; to receive	(4)
手段	shǒuduàn	measure, means	(13)
舒伯特	shūbótè	Schubert	(7)
舒曼	shūmàn	Schumann	(7)
书生	shūshēng	intellectual, scholar	(1)
属于	shǔyú	to belong to	(12)
帅	shuài	(to be) good-looking (male)	(2)
顺便	shùnbiàn	in passing	(3)
说服	shuōfú	to persuade	(3)
四重奏	sìchóngzòu	quartet	(7)
似乎	sìhū	to seem as if	(9)
思想	sīxiǎng	thought, thinking	(11)
寺院	sìyuàn	temple	(9)
素	sù	vegetable	(6)
俗话	súhuà	common saying	(4)
算了	suànle	Forget it!	(4)
随时	suíshí	at any time	(5)
随心所欲	suíxīnsuǒyù	to do whatever one wants	(9)
坦然地	tǎnránde	at ease, calmly	(1)
贪污	tānwū	embezzlement; to embezzle	(13)
特别	tèbié	specially; special	(6)
特点	tèdiǎn	characteristic	(7)
提到	tídào	to mention	(14)
提高	tígāo	to raise, to increase	(8)
提供	tígōng	to provide	(6)
提醒	tíxǐng	to remind	(4)
甜点	tiándiǎn	sweets	(6)
甜蜜	tiánmì	(to be) sweet	(9)
天下	tiānxià	in the world; the world	(7)
天真	tiānzhēn	(to be) naive, innocent	(4)
调整	tiáozhěng	to adjust	(5)

听从	tīngcóng	to obey	(10)
听觉	tīngjué	sense of hearing	(14)
痛苦	tòngkǔ	(to be) sad; suffering	(9)
童年	tóngnián	childhood	(1)
偷渡	tōudù	to secretly cross (e.g. seas)	(10)
头昏	tóuhūn	to be dizzy	(6)
偷懒	tōulǎn	to loaf on the job	(12)
偷窃	tōuqiè	to steal	(8)
投入	tóurù	to throw oneself into	(13)
投降	tóuxiáng	to surrender	(9)
突兀	túwù	(to be) abrupt	(14)
推辞	tuīcí	to decline	(6)
推荐	tuījiàn	to recommend	(7)
推销	tuīxiāo	to sell	(3)
推销员	tuīxiāoyuán	salesperson	(3)
推行	tuīxíng	to implement, to carry out	(13)
退休	tuìxiū	to retire	(8)
脱离	tuōlí	to get away from	(9)
完美	wánměi	(to be) perfect	(10)
玩弄	wánnòng	to play with	(9)
喂	wèi	to feed	(8)
伟大	wěidà	(to be) great	(2)
味道	wèidào	taste	(5)
味精	wèijīng	MSG	(6)
未来	wèilái	future	(11)
委屈	wěiqū	to feel wronged	(6)
危险	wēixiǎn	danger; (to be) dangerous	(4)
微笑	wēixiào	smile	(12)
唯一	wéiyī	only	(13)
位置	wèizhì	position	(10)
稳定	wěndìng	(to be) stable	(13)
文凭	wénpíng	diploma	(11)

握手	wòshǒu	to shake hands	(13)
无家可归	wújiākěguī	(to be) homeless	(10)
无精打采	wújīngdǎcǎi	to be spiritless	(13)
武器	wǔqì	weapon	(9)
席	xí	a number of (words)	(1)
牺牲	xīshēng	to sacrifice; sacrifice	(12)
细细（地）	xìxì	careful; carefully	(7)
息息相关	xīxīxiāngguān	(to be) closely related	(11)
吸引	xīyǐn	to attract	(3)
吸引力	xīyǐnlì	attraction, attractability	(3)
喜悦	xǐyuè	happiness	(14)
下定义	xià dìngyì	to give a definition	(9)
陷阱	xiànjǐng	trap	(9)
先秦	xiānqín	pre-Qin Dynasty period	(11)
羡慕	xiànmù	to admire	(7)
陷入	xiànrù	to fall into	(9)
限于	xiànyú	to be limited to	(12)
弦乐	xiányuè	string music	(7)
项	xiàng	measure word	(3)
相当	xiāngdāng	quite, reasonably	(14)
享受	xiǎngshòu	to enjoy; enjoyment	(3)
乡土	xiāngtǔ	countryside	(7)
享用	xiǎngyòng	to enjoy eating	(5)
象征	xiàngzhēng	to symbolize; symbol	(14)
萧邦	xiāobāng	Chopin	(7)
削减	xiāojiǎn	to reduce	(8)
小看	xiǎokàn	to look down	(14)
效率	xiàolǜ	efficiency	(8)
消失	xiāoshī	to disappear	(7)
小夜曲	xiǎoyèqǔ	serenade	(7)
协助	xiézhù	to assist	(8)
心得	xīndé	reflection	(14)

艺术	yìshù	art	(7)
一滩	yìtān	measure word for liquid	(7)
一头雾水	yìtóuwùshuǐ	to be totally confused	(12)
义务	yìwù	obligation	(13)
意义	yìyì	significance, meaning	(9)
一转眼	yìzhuǎnyǎn	in the blink of an eye	(11)
引起	yǐnqǐ	to cause	(1)
音效	yīnxiào	sound effects	(14)
阴影	yīnyǐng	shadow	(10)
音乐通	yīnyuètōng	expert in music	(7)
影射	yǐngshè	to allude to	(14)
影响	yǐngxiǎng	influence; to influence	(1)
营养	yíngyǎng	nutrition	(6)
营养不良	yíngyǎngbùliáng	(to be) malnourished	(6)
营造	yíngzào	to portray (in art, literature)	(14)
拥护	yōnghù	to support	(13)
拥有	yōngyǒu	to own	(12)
诱惑	yòuhuò	to seduce; seduction	(9)
有板有眼	yǒubǎnyǒuyǎn	(to be) rhythmical (in singing/speech)	(14)
有史以来	yǒushǐyǐlái	since the beginning of history	(3)
有效	yǒuxiào	to be effective	(3)
游行	yóuxíng	to parade; parade	(13)
有罪	yǒuzuì	guilty (of a crime)	(8)
与人为善	yǔrénwéishàn	to be kind to people	(1)
与书为友	yǔshūwéiyǒu	to treasure books as friends	(1)
预算	yùsuàn	budget	(8)
怨	yuàn	to blame	(4)
怨恨	yuànhèn	resentment and hatred	(14)
圆舞曲	yuánwǔqǔ	waltz	(7)
愿意	yuànyì	to be willing to	(4)
在野党	zàiyědǎng	party not in office	(13)
脏	zāng	(to be) dirty	(14)

早起晚睡	zǎoqǐwǎnshuì	to get up early and go to bed late	(4)
造谣	zàoyáo	to spread rumors	(13)
张狂	zhāngkuáng	to be insolent	(9)
真	zhēn	indeed, really	(1)
真理	zhēnlǐ	truth	(9)
振作	zhènzuò	to cheer up	(10)
争	zhēng	to fight, to argue	(4)
争宠	zhēngchǒng	to struggle to be favored	(14)
争风吃醋	zhēngfēngchīcù	to fight because of jealousy	(14)
政见	zhèngjiàn	political viewpoints	(13)
整天	zhěngtiān	all day long	(4)
征兆	zhēngzhào	sign	(13)
政治	zhèngzhì	politics	(13)
志	zhì	will, ideal	(11)
执法	zhífǎ	to enforce the law	(8)
芝麻(球)	zhīmá(qiú)	sesame (ball)	(6)
知识	zhīshí	knowledge	(1)
知识分子	zhīshífènzi	intellectual	(11)
职务	zhíwù	position	(2)
止息	zhǐxī	to stop	(9)
枝叶	zhīyè	leaf	(11)
直言不讳	zhíyánbúhuì	to speak bluntly	(6)
职业	zhíyè	occupation	(4)
知易行难	zhīyìxíngnán	to be easy to know and hard to do	(9)
知音	zhīyīn	close friend	(12)
执政党	zhízhèngdǎng	party in office	(13)
知足常乐	zhīzúchánglè	One is always happy if content with one's lot	(12)
忠实	zhōngshí	(to be) loyal	(8)
终于	zhōngyú	finally, in the end	(10)
赚	zhuàn	to earn, to make (money)	(4)
转	zhuǎn	to switch, to turn	(3)

LESSON ONE: CHILDHOOD

Objectives:

1. Develop students' ability to describe people.
2. Develop students' ability to support their statements with details.

Teaching Procedures and Techniques:

1. Students should study the lesson by themselves before class. However, they do not need to know all the supplementary new vocabulary. The teacher can check students' preparation by conducting dictation or asking comprehension questions about the lesson.

2. Students take turns describing/guessing the childhood experience of one person in the class. The description should consist of at least two parts, a) a general statement, such as, "he was very honest", and b) some specific hypothetical details to support the general statement.

3. After each description/guess, the person being described should either confirm or reject the description by providing specific examples or more details.

4. If none of the students wants to be the first person to be described, the teacher can volunteer to be the first person.

5. If there is more time, the class can spend time discussing the topics following the text.

Notes:

The teacher's role includes: 1) providing the necessary explanation and practicing the new vocabulary and grammar, 2) correcting students' errors without interrupting their discussion, 3) becoming a participant in the discussion.

LESSON TWO: DESCRIBING A PERSON

Objectives:

1. Develop students' ability to describe people.
2. Develop students' ability to express opinions.
3. Develop students' ability to support their statements with details.

Teaching Procedures and Techniques:

1. Students should study the lesson by themselves before class. However, they do not need to know all the supplementary new vocabulary. The teacher can check students' preparation by conducting dictation or asking comprehension questions about the lesson.

2. The teacher should lead the students in practicing the new patterns and words introduced in the lesson.

3. The teacher may show students a picture of a famous person and ask them to take turns describing the person's appearance, personality and so on. The description should consist of a general statement with some supporting details.

4. If students have different opinions about the person, the teacher should encourage debate among the students.

5. When the students have discussed the person sufficiently, the teacher should introduce another picture for the students to describe and talk about.

Notes:

1. The teacher should prepare at least 10 pictures of people that students all know and enjoy talking about (e.g. the president, the first lady, Confucius...)

2. In addition to participating in the discussion, the teacher should ask follow-up questions when students use new and difficult words to make sure that the students know the exact meaning of the new words. These follow-up questions are also useful for encouraging students to talk more and providing more supporting details.

LESSON THREE: MASTER SALESPERSON

Objectives:

  1. Develop students' ability to describe things.
  2. Develop students' ability to talk about popular products.
  3. Develop students' ability to persuade other people.

Teaching Procedures and Techniques:

  1. Students should study the lesson by themselves before class. The teacher can check the students' preparation by conducting dictation or asking comprehension questions about the lesson. The teacher can also encourage students to make sentences with the new words and sentence patterns, and ask one student to read aloud the sentence(s) as a dictation exercise for the rest of the class.

  2. The teacher leads the students practicing the new patterns and words in different meaningful contexts.

  3. Have students ask questions about the text, if they have any.

  4. Group students into pairs to practice the dialogue.

  5. Have students come to class with advertisements of their favorite products. (The teacher can provide some advertisements in Chinese for the students to choose from.) The teacher can conduct two activities: 1) pair work: one student tries to sell one thing to another student by describing it and trying to convince the other person to purchase it. The "consumer" should try to ask questions about the product, do some bargaining, or refuse to purchase it.; 2) small group work: one student tries to sell something to a group of people. The class can then decide who is the best salesperson.

Notes:

Students can use either Chinese or English advertisements, although they should be encouraged to use Chinese ones.

LESSON FOUR: EVERY FIELD OF WORK

Objectives:

1. Develop students' ability to describe what people do.
2. Develop students' ability to talk about the kind of job they like best.
3. Develop students' ability to talk about the advantages and disadvantages of different professions and occupations.

Teaching Procedures and Techniques:

1. Students should study the lesson by themselves before class. However, they don't need to know all the supplementary new words. The teacher can check students' preparation by conducting dictation or asking comprehension questions about the lesson. The teacher can also encourage students to make sentences with the new words and sentence patterns and ask one student to read aloud the sentence(s) as a dictation exercise for the rest of the class.

2. The teacher should encourage the students to practice the new patterns and words in different meaningful contexts. The teacher can begin at the sentence level and then move to paragraph level. Students should ask questions about the text, if they have any.

3. Ask students to take turns talking about their jobs: what they do, the nature of the job, and the advantages and disadvantages of this job. This report can be real or hypothetical. This exercise requires the students to prepare well before coming to the class.

4. When the student is done with the report, other people in the class can ask questions and continue to talk about the advantages and disadvantages of the job. The teacher should encourage students to use the new words and structures from the lesson and should keep bringing up interesting topics for discussion. All of this requires careful preparation on the part of the teacher.

Notes:

1. The teacher should also be a participant in the discussion so that students have a model to follow.

2. Students should be encouraged to use as many new words and structures as they can in the report and discussion of their jobs. Other students can join in the discussion by expressing their agreement or disagreement.

LESSON FIVE: PROBLEM-SOLVING

Objectives:

1. Develop students' ability to explain.
2. Develop students' ability with real-life problem-solving.

Teaching Procedures and Techniques:

1. Students should study the lesson by themselves before the class. The teacher can check students' preparation by conducting dictation or asking comprehension questions about the lesson. Students are encouraged to ask questions if they have difficulty understanding the texts.

2. The teacher leads the students in practicing the new patterns and words in different meaningful contexts.

3. In addition to the text, five more scenarios are designed for problem-solving (see text). Students should be well-prepared before coming to class. In class, they will be grouped into pairs to do the problem-solving exercises. Students can also choose their own conversation partners. Then, some pairs can be asked to do one of the problem-solving exercises in front of the class. As one pair does that, other students can offer assistance on either side.

4. After each scenario, the teacher and students can discuss the performance, point out what is not quite appropriate in the conversation, and offer advice on how to improve the problem-solving performance. Each scenario can be done more than once if necessary.

Notes:

1. In addition to being a facilitator and monitor of the conversations, the teacher can also be a participant. Unless the students stop to ask questions, the teacher should not interrupt the conversation. The teacher should take notes and do the correction and structural practice after the conversation is over.

2. Besides correcting students' errors in grammar and use of words, the teacher should also correct students if what they say is not socially appropriate. Students should learn how to do "code-switching" according to different social contexts.

LESSON SIX: LUNCH

Objectives:

1. Develop students' ability to describe things.
2. Develop students' ability to talk about their dietary habits.
3. Develop students' ability to support their opinions.

Teaching Procedures and Techniques:

1. Students should study the lesson by themselves before the class. However, they don't need to know all the supplementary new words. The teacher can check students' preparation by conducting dictation or asking comprehension questions about the lesson.

2. The teacher leads the students in practicing the new patterns and words in different meaningful contexts. The teacher can begin at the sentence level and then move to paragraph level.

3. Ask students to express their opinions about Miss Li's dietary habits. They can talk about whether they like her diet and why.

4. Put students in pairs of two and have them write a recipe for their favorite dish, which they then should present orally to the class. This practice will improve students' command of the listed text structure and words for food.

5. Activities for pairs of students: they are going to invite 5 or 6 friends to dinner, and are asked to make a list of the dishes they are going to serve, as well as a list of the ingredients they need to make the dishes.

6. Have students talk about the food service of their cafeteria and discuss topics given after the text of this lesson.

LESSON SEVEN: MUSIC

Objectives:

1. Develop students' ability to express abstract concepts.
2. Develop students' ability to talk about the music they enjoy listening to.

Teaching Procedures and Techniques:

1. Students should study the lesson by themselves before the class. The teacher can check the students' preparation by conducting dictation or asking comprehension questions about the lesson. Students are encouraged to ask questions if they have difficulty understanding the texts.

2. The teacher leads the students in practicing the new patterns and words in different meaningful contexts.

3. Students share their favorite music: each person plays 30-60 seconds of her or his music, talks about why it is good, and how the music relates to herself or himself. Other students in the class can ask questions or express their own opinions about the music.

4. The teacher can lead discussions on the topics following the text.

Notes:

1. The above activities require students to express abstract thinking and may be difficult for some of them. The teacher can start the discussion and provide a model for the students.

2. If there are students in the class who play a musical instrument, the teacher may ask her or him to play for a few minutes and then ask the class to discuss what they hear.

LESSON EIGHT: CRIME

Objectives:

1. Develop students' ability to express abstract concepts.
2. Develop students' ability to support their opinions.

Teaching Procedures and Techniques:

1. Students should study the lesson by themselves before coming to the class. The teacher can check students' preparation by conducting a dictation or asking comprehension questions about the lesson. Students are encouraged to ask questions if they have difficulty understanding the text.

2. The teacher leads the students in practicing the new patterns and words in different meaningful contexts.

3. The teacher leads a small group discussion. The following are two activities: 1) to finish what the judge would say in the text and then report to the class. Other people can ask questions about why they think the judge would say that; 2) to do the activity explained in the exercise section. Students should decide what the sentence should be for each of the criminal cases and explain why.